RUSSIA AND ARMS CONTROL: ARE THERE OPPORTUNITIES FOR THE OBAMA ADMINISTRATION?

Stephen J. Blank

March 2009

*****

Comments pertaining to this report are invited and should be forwarded to: Director, Strategic Studies Institute, U.S. Army War College, 122 Forbes Ave, Carlisle, PA 17013-5244.

*****

All Strategic Studies Institute (SSI) publications are available on the SSI homepage for electronic dissemination. Hard copies of this report also may be ordered from our homepage. SSI's homepage address is: *www.StrategicStudiesInstitute.army.mil.*

*****

The Strategic Studies Institute publishes a monthly e-mail newsletter to update the national security community on the research of our analysts, recent and forthcoming publications, and upcoming conferences sponsored by the Institute. Each newsletter also provides a strategic commentary by one of our research analysts. If you are interested in receiving this newsletter, please subscribe on our homepage at *www.StrategicStudiesInstitute.army.mil/newsletter/.*

ISBN 1-58487-381-7

CONTENTS

Foreword v
Summary vii
Introduction 1
Understanding the Current Impasse 17
    Russia 17
    America 25
Russia's Newly Announced Positions 37
Analyzing Russian Proposals 42
    The CFE Treaty 42
    The INF Treaty 53
    Tactical Nuclear Missiles 70
    Space Weapons 80
Missile Defenses 88
    Russian Replies to Missile Defenses 107
START and Russia's Strategic Challenges 111
Recommendations for the
    Obama Administration 118
Endnotes 140
About the Author...173

FOREWORD

As the Obama administration took office, Russo-American relations were generally acknowledged to be at an impasse. Arms control issues feature prominently in that conflicted agenda. Indeed, as of September 2008, the Bush administration was contemplating not just a break in arms talks but actual sanctions, and allowed the bilateral civil nuclear treaty with Russia to die in the Senate rather than go forward for confirmation. Russian spokesmen make clear their belief that American concessions on key elements of arms control issues like missile defenses in Europe are a touchstone for the relationship and a condition of any further progress towards genuine dialogue.

This impasse poses several risks beyond the obvious one of a breakdown in U.S.-Russian relations and the easily foreseeable bilateral consequences thereof. But those are by no means the only reasons for concern regarding the arms control agenda. Since the outbreak of the Russo-Georgian war in August 2008, both sides have further hardened positions and raised tensions apart from the war itself and Russia's quite evident refusal to abide by its own cease-fire terms. Nevertheless, and for better or worse, arms control and its agenda will remain at the heart of the bilateral Russo-American relationship for a long time. Arms control and disarmament issues are quintessentially political as well as military issues that are among the most critical components of the bilateral relationship and regional security in both Europe and Asia. For these reasons, neither the political nor the military aspect can be divorced from the other. And for these same reasons, we cannot refuse to participate in the bilateral effort to resolve those issues.

The Strategic Studies Institute is pleased to offer this monograph as part of the ongoing debate on Russo-American relations.

DOUGLAS C. LOVELACE, JR.
Director
Strategic Studies Institute

SUMMARY

Even before the Russian invasion of Georgia in August 2008, U.S.-Russian relations were reaching an impasse. Matters have only grown worse since then as Washington has stopped all bilateral military cooperation with Moscow, and it is difficult to imagine either Washington or the North Atlantic Treaty Organization (NATO) entering into arms control talks with Russia before the end of the George W. Bush administration. Indeed, as of September 2008, the administration is contemplating not just a break in arms talks but actual sanctions, and has allowed the bilateral civil nuclear treaty with Russia to die in the Senate rather than go forward for confirmation. U.S. Ambassador to Russia John Beyerle recently admitted that this is not a propitious time for bilateral nuclear cooperation and explicitly tied its resumption to Russian policy in Georgia. Similarly, Senator Richard Lugar (R-IN) and former Senator Sam Nunn (D-GA), who authored the Comprehensive Threat Reduction Program (CTR) to ensure the removal of unsafe nuclear materials and weapons from Russian arsenals, have expressed their concern that continuation of this vital program may now be in danger due to the deterioration in Russo-American relations. But those are by no means the only reasons for concern regarding the arms control agenda. Since August 8 when the war broke out, the following developments on both sides have further hardened positions and raised tensions apart from the war itself and Russia's quite evident refusal to abide by its own cease-fire terms.

Poland has signed an agreement with the United States to host up to 10 missile defense interceptors and, as a public sign of its distrust of NATO guarantees, demanded and obtained a mutual security guarantee and the stationing of *Patriot* air defense batteries from the United States, whose troops will defend some of those batteries through 2012. This triggered Russian threats to attack Poland with nuclear missiles and to "neutralize the American missile defenses by military means." Ukraine, undoubtedly due to Russian threats, has also stated its readiness to work with the West on missile defenses. Finally, Russia has announced its intention to equip the Baltic Fleet with nuclear weapons, and Swedish Foreign Minister Carl Bildt announced in return that "According to the information to which we have access, there are already tactical nuclear weapons in the Kaliningrad area. They are located both at and in the vicinity of units belonging to the Russia fleet."

For better or worse, arms control and its agenda remain at the heart of the bilateral Russo-American relationship and will remain there for a long time to come. Thus arms control and disarmament issues are quintessentially political as well as military issues that are among the most critical components of the bilateral relationship and regional security in both Europe and Asia. For these reasons, neither the political nor the military aspect can be divorced from the other. Furthermore, for the Russian government, the United States is its principal partner or interlocutor precisely because of the importance Moscow attaches to this agenda as having not just profound impact on the bilateral U.S.-Russian relationship, but as a major factor of global significance and import.

Accordingly, from Moscow's standpoint, trends in this bilateral relationship exercise a profound and fundamental influence upon the entire world order. Neither is this exclusively a Russian view. For example, Stephen Cimbala, a long-time analyst of the bilateral strategic relationship of U.S. and Russian military policies, writes that this relationship is one of complex interaction that relates to the strategic agenda of NATO and to the question not just of nuclear force structures among the superpowers, but also of global proliferation issues. This connection between the major nuclear powers' self-restraint and even downsizing of their arsenals and the viability and durability of the Nonproliferation Treaty (NPT) regime is clear and enshrined in both the NPT itself and in formal documents between Russia and America. For example, the Strategic Framework Declaration on U.S.-Russian relations signed by both Presidents Bush and Vladimir Putin on April 6, 2008, explicitly states that both governments will work toward a post-Strategic Arms Reduction Treaty (START) agreement on limiting strategic arms that would enable "strategic offensive arms reductions to the lowest possible level consistent with our national security requirements and alliance commitments." It also further stated that such an agreement would "be a further step in implementing our commitments under Article VI of the [Nonproliferation] Treaty." Under present conditions of hostility due to the crisis generated by the war in Georgia, the converse is true. If strategic arms control accords cannot be reached, the likelihood of increased proliferation increases accordingly, and the 2010 Review conference of the NPT will be as big a fiasco, if not worse, than was the 2005 session.

For these reasons, even if anyone is skeptical about many of the claims made on behalf of arms control and deterrence, certain hard facts and outcomes remain indisputable. Certainly for Russia, America's willingness to engage it seriously over these issues means that America respects it as a power and potential interlocutor, if not a partner. On the other hand, numerous and constant Russian complaints are that America will not respond to its proposals or consult with it. Although these are likely false claims, it has long been the case that the Bush administration's preference is to maximize its freedom of action by claiming that Russia and the United States were no longer enemies. Therefore we need not go back to the Cold War, and each side can pursue its own agenda in security.

The current discord on arms control reflects not only Moscow's wounded ego and foreign policy based to a considerable degree on feelings of resentment and revanche, but also America's unwillingness to take Russia as seriously as Moscow's inflated sense of grandiose self-esteem demands. If Russia and America reach a strategic impasse, the global situation as a whole deteriorates correspondingly.

Moreover, a constant factor in the relationship irrespective of its political temperature at any time is that both sides' nuclear forces remain frozen in a posture of mutual deterrence that implies a prior adversarial relationship that could easily deteriorate further under any and all circumstances. The problematic nature of the bilateral relationship is not due to deterrence. Rather, deterrence is a manifestation of a prior underlying and fundamental political antagonism in which Russia has settled upon deterrence as a policy and strategy because that strategy expresses its foundational presupposition of conflict with America and NATO. Thus the fundamental basis of the rivalry with Washington is political and stems from the nature of the Russian political system, which cannot survive in its present structure without that presupposition of conflict and enemies and a revisionist demand for equality with the United States so that it is tied down by Russian concerns and interests. From Russia's standpoint, the only way it can have security vis-à-vis the United States, given that presupposition of conflict, is if America is shackled to a continuation of the mutual hostage relationship, based on mutual deterrence that characterized the Cold War, so that it cannot act unilaterally. In this fashion, Russia gains a measure of restraint or even of control over U.S. policy. Thanks to such a mutual hostage relationship, Russian leaders see all other states who wish to attack them, or even to exploit internal crises like Chechnya, as being deterred. Therefore nuclear weapons remain a critical component in ensuring strategic stability and, as less openly stated, in giving Russia room to act freely in world affairs.

Indeed Moscow sees its nuclear arsenal as a kind of all-purpose deterrent that has deterred the United States and NATO from intervening in such conflicts as the Chechen wars. Nevertheless, its military and political leaders argue that threats to Russia are multiplying. Certainly Russian officials see the weaponization of space, the integration of space and terrestrial capabilities, missile defenses, the Reliable Replacement Weapons (RRW), and the U.S. global strike strategy as apart of a systematic, comprehensive strategy to threaten Russia. So in response Moscow must threaten Europe.

The perpetuation of the Cold War's mutual hostage relationship is, of course, exactly what the United States, at least under the George W. Bush administration, has striven mightily to leave behind. Russian analysts and officials believe in deterrence and the accompanying mutual hostage condition of both sides' nuclear forces as the only way to stop what they see as America's constant efforts to find ways in which nuclear weapons can be used for warfighting or to be free to use military force across the globe without being deterred by anyone. However, U.S. current weapon plans, the development of missile defenses, reluctance to negotiate verification protocols for a START treaty, NATO enlargement, and weapons in space, all suggest to Russia that there is "a growing gap between the military capabilities of the two countries. This gap challenges the condition of strategic parity that Russia still believes to be the underlying principle of its relationship with the United States. This enduring adversarial condition reflects a mutual failure on the part of both Washington and Moscow.

RUSSIA AND ARMS CONTROL:
ARE THERE OPPORTUNITIES FOR THE OBAMA
ADMINISTRATION?

INTRODUCTION

Even before the Russian invasion of Georgia in August 2008, U.S.-Russian relations were reaching an impasse. And matters have only grown worse since then as Washington has stopped all bilateral military cooperation with Moscow, and it is difficult to imagine either Washington or the North Atlantic Treaty Organization (NATO) entering into arms control talks with Russia before the end of the George W. Bush administration. Indeed, the administration is, as of September 2008, contemplating not just a break in arms talks but actual sanctions, and has allowed the bilateral civil nuclear treaty with Russia to die in the Senate rather than go forward for confirmation.[1] U.S. Ambassador to Russia John Beyerle recently admitted that this is not a propitious time for bilateral nuclear cooperation and explicitly tied its resumption to Russian policy in Georgia.[2] Similarly, Senator Richard Lugar (R-IN) and former Senator Sam Nunn (D-GA), who authored the Comprehensive Threat Reduction Program (CTR) to ensure the removal of unsafe nuclear materials and weapons from Russian arsenals, have expressed their concern that continuation of this vital program may now be in danger due to the deterioration in Russo-American relations.[3] More recently, as a result of the U.S. presidential election and the inability of the United States to respond effectively to the invasion of Georgia and truncation of its integrity, arms control negotiations have resumed. Indeed, Moscow has repeatedly made

1

clear its desire to negotiate with President Obama on all the outstanding arms control issues.[4]

But despite the resumption of talks, there are still many reasons for concern regarding the arms control agenda. Since August 8 when the war broke out, the following developments on both sides have further hardened positions and raised tensions apart from the war itself and Russia's quite evident refusal to abide by its own cease-fire terms.

Poland has signed an agreement with the United States to host up to 10 missile defense interceptors and, as a public sign of its distrust of NATO guarantees, demanded and obtained a mutual security guarantee and the stationing of Patriot air defense batteries from the United States, whose troops will defend some of those batteries through 2012. This, in turn, triggered Russian threats to attack Poland with nuclear missiles and to "neutralize the American missile defenses by military means.[5] Ukraine, too, undoubtedly due to Russian threats, has also stated its readiness to work with the West on missile defenses.[6] Finally, Russia has announced its intention to equip the Baltic Fleet with nuclear weapons and Swedish Foreign Minister Carl Bildt announced in return that, "According to the information to which we have access, there are already tactical nuclear weapons in the Kaliningrad area. They are located both at and in the vicinity of units belonging to the Russia fleet."[7]

In other words, Bildt disclosed that Russia has long been violating the Presidential Nuclear Initiatives agreed to by Presidents George H. W. Bush and Boris Yeltsin removing tactical nuclear weapons (or nonstrategic nuclear weapons as Moscow calls them, TNW and NSNW respectively) from on board their countries' fleets in 1991-92. This public revelation of Russian cheating would, under the best of circumstances, have raised red flags in Washington and Europe regarding future cooperation. Today it merely confirms the gathering and overwhelming impression that arms control deals with Russia are inherently dangerous and futile because Moscow will not abide by them unless there is a rigorous inspection and verification regime.

Furthermore, General Nikolai Makarov, Russia's Chief of the General Staff, has recently publicly stated that Russia will retain its TNW as long as Europe is "packed with armaments" as a guarantee of Russian security and that priority funding will be directed to Russia's nuclear arsenal.[8] Beyond that, Russia is buying new nuclear missiles whose main attribute is their ability to evade U.S. missile defenses and, as part of its prioritization of its nuclear forces, will buy and deliver to the forces over 70 strategic missiles, over 30 short-range *Iskander* missiles, and a large number of booster rockets and aircraft.[9] Moscow will also spend $35.3 billion on serial production of all weapons in 2009-11 (1 trillion rubles) and virtually double the number of strategic missile launches to 13 for 2009.[10] This procurement policy represents both a quantum leap in Russian capabilities if it can be consummated and also would constitute a major step in a new action-reaction cycle of procurements based on the old Cold War paradigm. The key question is whether the Russian economy, which is now reeling under the shock of what will almost certainly be a protracted and global economic crisis, can sustain this level of procurement without collapsing as did its Soviet predecessor. This testifies to the possibility that recognition of the strain upon the economy inherent in such ambitious procurement goals, along with the desire to enter into a serious negotiation with the Obama administration, may be affecting policy considerations. Colonel-General Nikolai Solovtsov, Commander in Chief of Russia's Strategic Missile Forces, also recently stated that, "If Americans give up plans to deploy the third positioning region (i.e., missile defenses in Poland and the Czech Republic — author) and other elements of the strategic missile defense system, then certainly we will adequately respond to it."[11]

Therefore, the current arms control agenda stands poised between a continued hardening of both sides' positions or else the possibility of substantive negotiations. Likewise, for better or worse, arms control and its agenda remain at the heart of the bilateral Russo-American relationship and will remain there for a long time to come. Thus arms control and disarmament issues are quintessentially political as well as military issues that are among the most critical components of the bilateral relationship and regional security in both Europe and Asia. For these reasons, neither the political nor the military aspect can be divorced from the other. Furthermore, for the Russian government, the United States is its principal partner or interlocutor precisely because of the importance Moscow attaches to this agenda as having not just profound impact on the bilateral U.S.-Russian relationship, but as a major factor of global significance and import. As Russian Chief of Staff General Yuri Baluyevsky wrote in 2006, "It will not be an exaggeration to say that the relations between Russia and the United States have actually defined and are defining the situation in the world over the course of nearly an entire century now."[12]

Accordingly, from Moscow's standpoint, trends in this bilateral relationship exercise a profound and fundamental influence upon the entire world order. Neither is this exclusively a Russian view. For example, Stephen Cimbala, a long-time analyst of the bilateral strategic relationship of U.S. and Russian military policies, writes that this relationship is one of complex interaction that relates to the strategic agenda of NATO and to the question not just of nuclear force structures among the superpowers, but also of global proliferation issues.[13] This connection between the major nuclear powers' self-restraint and even downsizing of their arsenals and the viability and durability of the Nonproliferation Treaty (NPT) regime is clear and enshrined in both the NPT itself and in formal documents between Russia and America. For example, the Strategic Framework Declaration on U.S.-Russian relations signed by both Presidents Bush and Vladimir Putin on April 6, 2008, explicitly states that both governments will work toward a post-Strategic Arms Reduction Treaty (START) agreement on limiting strategic arms that would enable "strategic offensive arms reductions to the lowest possible level consistent with our national security requirements and alliance commitments." It also further stated that such an agreement would "be a further step in implementing our commitments under Article VI of the [Nonproliferation] Treaty."[14] Under present conditions of hostility due to the crisis generated by the war in Georgia, the converse is true. If strategic arms control accords cannot be reached, the likelihood of increased proliferation increases accordingly, and the 2010 Review conference of the Nonproliferation Treaty (NPT) will be as big a fiasco, if not worse, than was the 2005 session.

For these reasons, even if one, like this author, is skeptical about many of the claims made on behalf of arms control and deterrence, certain hard facts and outcomes remain indisputable. Certainly for Russia,

America's willingness to engage it seriously over these issues means that America respects it as a power and potential interlocutor, if not a partner. On the other hand, numerous and constant Russian complaints are that America will not respond to its proposals, consult with it, etc. Although these are likely false claims, it has long been the case that the Bush administration's preference is to maximize its freedom of action by claiming that (at least until now) Russia and the United States were no longer enemies. Therefore we need not go back to the Cold War, and each side can pursue its own agenda in security. Furthermore, as President Bush has consistently argued since 2001,

> I am committed to achieving a credible deterrent with the lowest possible number of nuclear weapons consistent with our national security needs, including our obligations to our allies. My goal is to move quickly to reduce nuclear forces. The United States will lead by example to achieve our interests and the interests for peace in the world.[15]

The current discord on arms control reflects not only Moscow's wounded ego and foreign policy based to a considerable degree on feelings of resentment and revanche, but also America's unwillingness to take Russia as seriously as Moscow's inflated sense of grandiose self-esteem demands.[16] But even if Moscow's constant need of reassurance is invariably affronted by governments who refuse to accept its inflated demands for compensation and status, it is still the case that the bilateral strategic relationship is a factor of enormous consequence in international affairs beyond their own bilateral relationship. If Russia and America reach a strategic impasse, the global situation as a whole deteriorates correspondingly.

Moreover, a constant factor in the relationship irrespective of its political temperature at any time is that both sides' nuclear forces remain frozen in a posture of mutual deterrence that implies a prior adversarial relationship that could easily deteriorate further under any and all circumstances.[17] This point is critical. The problematic nature of the bilateral relationship, just as was the case during the Cold War — albeit less intensely today — is not due to deterrence. Rather, deterrence is a manifestation of a prior underlying and fundamental political antagonism in which Russia has settled upon deterrence as a policy and strategy because that strategy expresses its foundational presupposition of conflict with America and NATO.[18] Thus the fundamental basis of the rivalry with Washington is political and stems from the nature of the Russian political system which cannot survive in its present structure without that presupposition of conflict, enemies, and a revisionist demand for equality with the United States so that it is tied down by Russian concerns and interests. From Russia's standpoint, the only way it can have security vis-à-vis the United States, given that presupposition of conflict, is if America is shackled to a continuation of the mutual hostage relationship based on mutual deterrence that characterized the Cold War, so that it cannot act unilaterally. In this fashion, to the degree that both sides are shackled to this mutual hostage relationship, Russia gains a measure of restraint or even of control over U.S. policy. For as Patrick Morgan has observed, this kind of classic deterrence "cuts through the complexities" of needing to have a full understanding of or dialogue with the other side. Instead, it enables a state, in this case Russia, to "*simplify by dictating*, the opponent's preferences."[19] (Italics in the original) Thanks to such a mutual hostage relationship,

Russian leaders see all other states who wish to attack them or even to exploit internal crises like Chechnya as being deterred. Therefore nuclear weapons remain a critical component in ensuring strategic stability and, as less openly stated, in giving Russia room to act freely in world affairs.[20]

Indeed Moscow sees its nuclear arsenal as a kind of all-purpose deterrent that has deterred the United States and NATO from intervening in such conflicts as the Chechen wars. Nevertheless, its military and political leaders, e.g., Colonel-General Nikolai Solovtsov, Commander in Chief of the Strategic Missile (Rocket) Forces, argue that threats to Russia are multiplying. Thus Solovtsov recently argued that,

> Some potential threats to the defense and security of the Russian Federation, including large-scale ones, remain, and in some sectors are intensifying. Moreover, the possibility cannot be ruled out that major armed conflict could arise near Russia's borders, which will affect its security interests, or that there could be a direct military threat to our country's security. This is graphically illustrated by the military aggression unleashed by Georgia overnight from 7 to 8 August against South Ossetia.[21]

While such statements represent the fantasy world of the Russian military where threats are always rising despite the plain evidence of Western demilitarization and omit to mention that Georgia neither attacked Russia nor in fact started the war that was a Russian provocation, his remarks do amply underscore the importance of deterrence and the permanent sense of being under threat that drives Russian policy. Hence the need for deterrence, primarily, though not exclusively, of the United States at the price of accepting that Russia, too, is deterred from a nuclear strike on the United States. In return for accepting that it, too, is similarly deterred, Russia, however, postulates as one of the fundamental corollaries of its policy and strategy that Moscow must retain a capability to intimidate and destroy Europe with its nuclear and other missiles. Hence the continuing aforementioned reliance upon TNW no matter the cost. In other words, believing a priori that Europe is the site of a presumptive enemy action against it, Russia demands as a condition of its security that the rest of Europe be insecure. Indeed, reports of Russia's forthcoming defense doctrine openly state that the United States and NATO represent the main threats to Russian security and that Washington will continue to seek military supremacy and disregard international law for a generation. Furthermore, unlike the United States, Russia is engaged in a comprehensive modernization and renewal of all of its nuclear weapons, clearly in the belief that it needs to deter America by military means, and maybe even fight using such weapons. Likewise, Moscow has consistently said that the deployment of U.S. missile defenses in Europe and Asia will disrupt existing balances of strategic forces and undermine global and regional stability.[22] There is also conflicting evidence as to whether or not Russia intends to tie completion of a treaty on strategic missiles reduction with the removal of missile defenses from Central and Eastern Europe.[23] In addition, Russia's leaders openly contend that one cannot discuss European security without taking into account the missile defense issue or the Conventional Forces in Europe (CFE) Treaty.[24] Certainly Russian officials see the weaponization of space, the integration of space and terrestrial capabilities, missile defenses, the Reliable Replacement Weapons (RRW), and the U.S. global strike strategy as a part of a systematic, comprehensive strategy to threaten Russia. So in response Moscow must threaten Europe. Indeed, Foreign Minister Sergei Lavrov recently repeated the now habitual but no less mendacious charge that missile defenses in Europe, systems that allegedly used to be regulated by bilateral agreements to maintain parity, are now being introduced close to Russia's borders, thereby rupturing that parity in Europe and elsewhere.[25] During his recent trip to Poland, Lavrov went even further, saying that,

> For many decades, the basis for strategic stability and security in the world was parity between Russia and the United States in the sphere of strategic offensive and defensive arms. However, in recent years, the U.S. Administration chose a course towards upsetting that parity and gaining a unilateral advantage in the strategic domain. Essentially it's not just about global missile defense. We also note that the U.S. has been reluctant to stay within the treaties on strategic offensive arms, and that it is pursuing the Prompt Global Strike concept, and developing projects to deploy strike weapons in outer space. This, understandably, will not reinforce the security of Europe or of Poland itself.[26]

Lavrov then went on to say that if Poland, under the circumstances, chose a "special allied relationship" with Washington, then it would have to bear the responsibilities and risks involved and that Moscow, in principle, opposed having its relations with third parties being a function of Russian-American disputes.[27]

Thus Russia's arms control posture also represents its continuing demand for substantive, if not quantitative, parity as well as for deterrence with a perceived adversarial United States in order to prevent Washington from breaking free of the Russian embrace and following policies that Russia deems antithetical to its interests.[28] Moreover, that parity is calculated not just globally, but in regional balances as well so that Russia also demands a qualitative or substantive parity with America at various regional levels, most prominently Europe. Russia's demand for restoring parity at both the global and regional levels entails not an unreachable numerical parity, but rather a strategic stability or equilibrium where both sides' forces remain mutually hostage to each other in a deterrent relationship and where the United States cannot break free to pursue its global or regional interests unilaterally, or what Moscow calls unilaterally. For example, up to December 2008, the two sides have failed to reach agreement on a reduction of strategic weapons because they cannot even agree as to what constitutes a strategic weapon. Because the Bush administration wants to get away from using nuclear weapons and has so stated in its public rhetoric, and because the United States is no longer producing any nuclear weapons, it insists on confining the treaty to strategic (intercontinental ballistic missiles [ICBMs] or sea-launched ballistic missiles [SLBMs]) offensive nuclear weapons that are actually deployed while retaining the possibility of several hundred or thousand so-called "operational reserve" weapons that are not physically deployed and may eventually be dismantled. This would allow the United States to conduct its strategy of having a prompt global (conventional) strike capability and to mount conventional ballistic or cruise missiles on board launchers, including submarines, hitherto reserved for nuclear launches. For Russia, such conventional missiles with a global range are inherently strategic weapons, and they want both those missiles (which, after all, represent an innovation in U.S. strategy), as well as the reserve nuclear weapons, counted in any strategic weapons treaty and thereby banned. Until this issue is resolved, no treaty is likely to come out of the current negotiating process.[29] And Moscow's stance openly reflects its commitment to its understanding of strategic stability under contemporary conditions, i.e., no innovations for the United States even as it works on many of these selfsame projects.

Moreover, as Lavrov's remarks imply, Russia demands a free hand vis-à-vis European states so that it can maximize the leverage it can bring to bear upon its relationships with them. This leverage very clearly includes the nuclear leverage it gains by being able to intimidate them with either conventional or nuclear missiles. Russia wants to relate to key countries and regions irrespective of its relations with America so that it can have this free hand in regard to them and thus resents the presence of American power in Europe, Asia, etc. Indeed, not only does it wish to shackle U.S. power to the mutual hostage relationship of mutual deterrence and thus mutually agreed destruction (MAD), it also clearly believes, as Lavrov's and dozens of other threats to Poland and other states show, that its security remains contingent upon its ability to intimidate Europe with nuclear weapons and threats.

The perpetuation of the Cold War's mutual hostage relationship is, of course, exactly what the United States, at least under the George W. Bush administration, has striven mightily to leave behind. Indeed, the Russian views outlined below confirm Ambassador Linton Brooks' assertion that "arms control is for adversaries," and typifies the Bush administration's approach to arms control.[30] Russian analysts and officials believe in deterrence and the accompanying mutual hostage condition of both sides' nuclear forces as the only way to stop what they see as America's constant efforts to

12

find ways in which nuclear weapons can be used for warfighting or to be free to use military force across the globe without being deterred by anyone. Russia also seeks thereby to ensure that it possesses a substantive measure of control over any and all escalation processes. Therefore any advance—low-yield nuclear weapons, weaponization of space, the RRW, missile defenses, use of Trident conventional missiles on a nuclear launcher, etc.—that could give Washington ideas of having a real chance to use such weapons or to have a real first-strike capability that can sufficiently degrade Russia's nuclear capabilities to the point of inhibiting a retaliatory strike as called for by deterrence theory must be stopped in its tracks.[31] And this is true even though Moscow, as we shall see below, is working on almost all of these issues itself. In addition, therefore, the primary mission or top military priority of the government is maintenance of its nuclear forces and is a condition of fighting ability and readiness, i.e., deterrence.[32]

However, U.S. current weapon plans, the development of missile defenses, reluctance to negotiate verification protocols for a START treaty, NATO enlargement, and weapons in space, all suggest to Russia that there is "a growing gap between the military capabilities of the two countries. This gap challenges the condition of strategic parity that Russia still believes to be the underlying principle of its relationship with the United States."[33] This enduring adversarial condition reflects a mutual failure on the part of both Washington and Moscow. The extent of this failure can be summarized in the following points:

- Even before Georgia, there were no genuine arms control negotiations between Russia and the United States, only "consultations," mostly on antiballistic missile (ABM) problems without real prospects for success;

- The ABM treaty does not work any more, which means that in this field there is no kind of legal limitation on any sort of ABM activities;
- The CFE treaty practically does not work; Russia suspended its participation in this treaty for an indefinite period of time. Moreover, after Georgia, it probably is dead;
- The START-1 Treaty will expire in December 2009, and the parties must give notice of an intention to renew by December 5, 2008, something that is quite unlikely in the present atmosphere;
- The START-2 Treaty did not enter into legal force;
- The Strategic Offensive Treaty Reductions (SORT) Treaty (The Moscow Treaty of 2002) still works, but this agreement does not provide for any kind of verification and control measures. And when the START treaty expires, there will be no mechanism at all for mutual verification and confidence;
- With regard to the Intermediate Range Nuclear Forces (INF) Treaty, the question of a possible withdrawal of Russia as a response to the U.S. ABM deployment in Europe is raised at different levels of the Russian government as a matter of course. Given the crisis growing out of Georgia, it too could become a treaty that Russia abandons.
- The NPT regime is widely believed to be in danger of falling apart;
- The 1972 Convention on the Prohibition of Biological and Toxin Weapons still does not

have a verification system because the U.S. Government will not sign the verification protocol, believing it to be ineffective in preventing violations (the Soviet Union violated this accord on a grand scale);

- The 1997 Protocol on the Prohibition of Chemical Weapons will not be implemented according to its schedule by the United States and Russia for financial reasons.[34]

And presently the official position of all the declared nuclear states except North Korea may be systematized, as Alexei Arbatov has done, in the following manner.

- All of them envision the use of nuclear weapons in response to a nuclear attack;
- All, except China, plan for first use of nuclear weapons in response to an attack with chemical or biological weapons;
- All, except China and India, imply the first use of nuclear weapons in response to an overwhelming attack with conventional forces against oneself or one's allies;
- All, except China and India, may initiate the use of nuclear weapons to preempt or prevent an attack with missiles or other delivery systems of weapons of mass destruction (WMD);
- The United States envisions the use of nuclear weapons in various other contingencies if necessary;
- Russia may decide to selectively initiate the use of nuclear weapons to "deescalate an aggression" or to "demonstrate resolve," as well as to respond to a conventional attack on its nuclear forces, command, control, communications, and intelligence (C3I) forces

(including satellites), atomic power plants, and other nuclear targets.[35]

In this context of lack of progress on arms control, Moscow also charges that Washington will not negotiate with it seriously because Washington opposes any restrictions "on weapons delivery hardware and nuclear warhead storage," i.e., the ability to keep weapons in reserve, and will only limit actual deployments. Russia wants to subject the total volume and quantity of nuclear arms on both sides to reduction. Equally disconcerting to Moscow is the fact that Washington will not follow former President Putin's logic and jointly discuss threats with it (a procedure that would, or so Moscow hopes, give it a restraining hand on U.S. force developments).[36] At the same time other U.S. writers charge that Russia and China are busily modernizing their nuclear weapons and infrastructure while America is essentially sitting on its decaying nuclear bayonets and refraining from such modernization. They therefore project that if this posture continues into the future, America will be weaker in strategic power than Russia, a condition that will shred our alliances and extended deterrence, giving other states freer reign abroad to threaten American interests.[37] Obviously this situation would constitute a recipe for future political struggle that could easily tip over in any one of the many contested zones of world politics into actual armed conflict, an inherently unstable condition where forces exist to deter each other based on a mutual presupposition of future conflict.[38] Thus, beyond the impasse, we confront the real possibility of a renewed nuclear arms race.

UNDERSTANDING THE CURRENT IMPASSE

Russia.

In Russia's case we can attribute the current impasse to persisting Soviet mentalities, structure of government, and policies carried over to the present. Indeed, this author has argued that, from Moscow's side, this adversarial posture derives inherently from the autocratic, regressive, and neo-Tsarist structure of its government.[39] But that factor is then reinforced by its perception of American policies. As Moscow grows more autocratic at home, aggressive in its policies, and more truculent in its rhetoric, it is increasingly dominated by a threat perception based on its inability to imagine a world without the presupposition of conflict and threat and the frank admission of its adversarial relationship with Washington even as it offers strategic partnership, as in its new foreign policy concept.[40]

Moscow thus discerns or claims to discern dawning threats from U.S. and/or NATO military power even though in actual fact today it has the most benign threat environment in its history. For example, Lieutenant General V. A. Gusachenko wrote in the General Staff's Journal, *Voyennaya Mysl'* (*Military Thought*), that Russia faces real threats to its security "in practically all spheres of its vital activities."[41] He is not alone in arguing this way. Solovtsov recently said that,

> Some potential threats to the defense and security of the Russian Federation, including large-scale ones, remain, and in some sectors, are intensifying. Moreover, the possibility cannot be ruled out that major armed conflicts could arise near Russia's borders which will affect its security interests, or that there could be a direct military

threat to our country's security. This is graphically illustrated by the military aggression unleashed by Georgia overnight from 7 to 8 August against South Ossetia.[42]

It is notable that Solovtsov, who in this is representative of both the political and military elite, omits the fact that on August 7-8, 2008, and even now, South Ossetia was recognized by everyone, including Russia, as Georgian territory. Hence there was never any threat to Russia from Georgia. Apart from confirming Russian threat perceptions and Moscow's propensity to manufacture wholly fabricated threats, he thus also suggests the enduring imperial drive in Russian thinking that contributes so much to its presupposition of being in a state of ongoing conflict with its neighbors. Nevertheless, Solovtsov, not surprisingly, also argues that new military uses for nuclear weapons are coming into being. Thus,

> The radical changes that have occurred since the end of the Cold War in international relations and the considerable reduction of the threat that a large-scale war, even more so a nuclear one, could be unleashed, have contributed to the fact that in the system of views on the role of nuclear arms both in Russia and the U.S., a political rather than military function has begun to prevail. In relation to this, besides the traditional forms and methods in the combat use of the RVSN [Russian Strategic Rocket Forces], a new notion "special actions" by the groupings of strategic offensive arms has emerged. . . . Such actions mean the RVSN's containment actions, their aim to prevent the escalation of a high-intensity non-nuclear military conflict against the Russian Federation and its allies.[43]

In other words, though there is no threat or a diminishing threat of large-scale war, a new use for nuclear weapons will be their use in actions during such a war to control intrawar escalation. It is not surprising that Solovtsov is arguing for increasing the forces under his command, but it also is the case that such dialectical reasoning makes no sense unless one postulates an a priori hostility between East and West and grants Russia the right of deterrence that it has unilaterally arrogated to itself over other states who have never publicly accepted it. Indeed, the new calls for renovating the nuclear forces and having a solution guaranteeing nuclear deterrence in all cases has now become policy even if America deploys its global defense system and moves to a defense dominant world.[44]

Putin's authoritative remarks as president further augmented and developed these trends in Russian thinking. In his speeches since 2006, Putin repeatedly charged that NATO enlargement, missile defenses, the incitement of terrorism, growing American military emplacement in Central and Eastern Europe, refusal to submit to the United Nations (UN) on questions of using force, calls for democracy in Russia, militarization of space, use of conventional missiles in intercontinental ballistic missiles (ICBMs), development of the Reliable Replacement Warhead (RRW), the use of low-yield nuclear weapons or of conventional missiles atop nuclear launchers for missions hitherto described as nuclear, other new weapons, and the militarization of space all present threats to Russia. These reputedly aim at coercing and marginalizing Russia by means of threats against its vital interests and are allegedly drawing closer to Russia's borders.[45]

Reflecting that presupposition of entrenched East-West hostility, Foreign Minister Sergei Lavrov told an interviewer in February 2007 that,

> Our main criterion is ensuring the Russian Federation's security and maintaining strategic stability as much as possible. . . . We have started such consultations already. I am convinced that we need a substantive discussion on how those lethal weapons could be curbed on the basis of mutual trust and balance of forces and interests. We will insist particularly on this approach. We do not need just the talk that we are no longer enemies and therefore we should not have restrictions for each other. This is not the right approach. It is fraught with an arms race, in fact, because, it is very unlikely that either of us will be ready to lag behind a lot.[46]

Here Lavrov signaled Russia's unwillingness to leave a mutually adversarial relationship with America and its presupposition of mutual hostility as reflected in both sides' nuclear deployments. Similarly Alexei Arbatov ridicules the administration's view, stated above by Ambassador Brooks, that because the two sides are no longer adversaries, detailed arms control talks are no longer necessary, as either naiveté or outright hypocrisy.[47] Nevertheless, whatever the failures of the Bush administration are or have been, and they are discussed below, any objective analysis of Russian policy would concede that the Russian elite had hardened its position on America by 2000 and that Putin's shift to support after September 11, 2001 (9/11) reflected his personal view, which was clearly not internalized by his subordinates.[48] Thus the overwhelming inertia of the Russian state and of its policies is and was anti-American. And as Washington pursued policies that increasingly seemed to confirm the validity of that anti-American perspective, Putin gradually moved to embrace it.

Furthermore, the continuing failure of its conventional forces to reform to meet the demands of the times and of its defense industry to prepare either enough or enough quality weapons for these forces leaves Moscow with a defense force that is too weighted in the direction of threats towards rapid escalation to first-strike threats, if not use of nuclear weapons as Solovtsov hinted above.[49] Yet as we shall see below, it cannot provide enough nuclear weapons by 2015 to obtain anything more than a state of minimum deterrence. Indeed, its forces are already configured at that level. Thus all of its military options, for all of the boasting about of long-range bomber patrols, claiming territory in the Arctic, buzzing American ships, and now talking about bases for its long-range and nuclear capable bombers in Cuba, as Russian analysts realize, are, to a considerable degree, rhetoric for domestic consumption. Under the circumstances (and until the economic realities generated by the global crisis that erupted in 2007-08 make themselves felt), Russia is not only committed to an extensive conventional rearmament, but to a thoroughgoing nuclear one as well.[50] And its recent exercises, most notably Stabilnost' 2008 (Stability 2008) reflect preparation for scenarios entailing the actual use of nuclear weapons in a war.[51]

In fact, and Russia's leaders know it well, Russia's defense industry cannot meet the state's demands for serial or quality production of high-precision conventional weapons that alone would justify its remaining a major conventional power, and its army, which refuses to become truly professional, is hardly able (except for some niche specialties) to conduct high-tech operations and use that equipment to optimal effect.[52] Although it can overwhelm countries in the Commonwealth of Independent States (CIS) like Georgia, conflicts with stronger military powers present a rather different picture and problems for Moscow.

And beyond that series of causes, we find that Russia, laboring under these conditions, has long considered the main strategic mission of its nuclear forces to be one of guaranteeing deterrence against aggression, a posture that has been reiterated to both Russian defense and political elites and to NATO.[53] In addition, that deterrence posture is openly advertised as being directed against NATO, and this too has long been the case. As First Deputy Foreign Minister Alexander Avdeyev wrote in 1999,

> Cautiousness in the sense of understanding what the present day NATO is, and alertness because a military aggression occurred in Europe (the Kosovo operation of 1999—author) [is necessary]. What are we to do in the future? Of course, we cannot increase our military power to equal the aggregate military power of all NATO member states. We would not be able to bear such an enormous burden. But the Russian military doctrine must proceed from the fact that Russia must adequately deter the adversary, and that it must have armed forces at such a level that will avert attack by any country. The same applies to politicians in NATO who could be carried away and have military intentions towards Russia.[54]

Similarly, arguing against the continuing posture of mutual nuclear deterrence that characterizes (at least in Moscow's eyes) the bilateral strategic relationship, Sergei Kortunov writes that,

> The situation of mutual nuclear deterrence—even minimal nuclear deterrence—in fact is in flagrant contradiction both with the proclaimed idea of a partnership and with the idea of international security.

No matter what kind of incredible efforts would be undertaken at the high political level in order to break away from the boundaries of the Cold War, the situation of mutual nuclear deterrence, which was materialized in the military potentials, is theoretically capable of reproducing all of the aggregate of confrontation(al) interstate relations at any moment.[55]

Today Kortunov's warnings have materialized in reality. Indeed, in 2007 Putin virtually heralded the return of a Cold War-type arms race in the face of American missile defenses in Europe when he told a press conference of G-8 country reporters that Russia and the West were returning to the Cold War and added that,

Of course, we will return to those times. And it is clear that if part of the U.S. nuclear capability is situated in Europe and that our military experts consider that they represent a potential threat, then we will have to take appropriate retaliatory steps. What steps? Of course, we must have new targets in Europe. And determining precisely which means will be used to destroy the installations that our experts believe represent a potential threat for the Russian Federation is a matter of technology. Ballistic or cruise missiles or a completely new system. I repeat that it is a matter of technology.[56]

No less consequential than the observation about returning to the Cold War is the fact that Putin here stated that he has bought the General Staff's vision and version of ubiquitous a priori American and Western threats expressed in a worst-case scenario. Worse yet, he openly conceded their power to define and formulate those threats and on that basis formulate requirements for defense policy and strategy. Indeed, here he openly invited the General Staff—these military experts—to determine Russia's threat assessment and announced that the government would accept it. Not surprisingly, that assessment of the Russian military, running true to its traditions, is alarmist and based on inflated versions of the worst-case scenario. Therefore, for Moscow, not only is arms control necessary because of a priori perception of an inherently adversarial relationship with America, its forces are also configured in a way according primacy to the mission of deterrence that also presupposes a potential armed conflict with America, making both sides' nuclear forces reenact the mutual hostage relationship of the Cold War.

Furthermore, Russia wants to keep things this way because any unilateral, substantive, or qualitative progress in American capabilities beyond the confines of what Russia defines as strategic stability will allow America to harvest the full benefits of the Revolution in Military Affairs (RMA) and give it either a means of attacking Russia's nuclear arsenal, nullifying it by missile defenses, bypassing it by high-precision conventional attacks, or combining the three through space weaponization. Such capabilities need not be used in conflict to be successful, all they need to do is be deployed as instruments of coercive diplomacy as in a Kosovo-type crisis, one of the many nightmare scenarios of the Russian leadership. And the nightmare is, as countless Russian statements state openly, that the parity with the United States will then no longer exist.[57]

Weapons in space, the use of conventional missiles on nuclear launchers, and missile defenses, are among such breakout possibilities for America. As Pavel Podvig has observed,

> One of the consequences of this is that if the promises held by the revolution in military affairs materialize,

24

even incompletely, they may significantly lower the threshold of military intervention. And this is exactly the outcome that Russia is worried about, for it believes that the new capabilities might open the way to a more aggressive interventionist policy of the United States and NATO, that may well challenge Russia's interests in various regions and especially in areas close to the Russian borders.[58]

America.

Nonetheless, and as a result of Russia's nuclear bluster and overall belligerently anti-American policy, the Pentagon has now responded with its own determination to ensure the quality and responsiveness of America's nuclear deterrent.[59] Indeed, even before the war with Georgia, the Navy was considering the possibility of deploying *Aegis* warship patrols in the Baltic or Black Seas (the latter would be a violation of the Montreux Convention of 1936 and Ankara, not to mention Moscow, would never allow it in peacetime) to protect missile defense sites in Poland and the Czech Republic since they might become the first targets in a phased enemy attack.[60] Similarly, Navy spokesmen are now writing and talking about "hedging our bets vis-à-vis Russia" and its drive to rearm. This also includes possible future naval missions with regard to ensuring energy supplies across Central Asia and the Caucasus. In a related vein, we see concern as to what the future Russian Navy will be, and we should remember that it will be primarily a nuclear oriented Navy.

> While current capability and intent pose no immediate danger, we should be wise to remember that China wasted no time in translating its conversion-to-capitalism-affluence into a navy that poses a serious challenge to U.S. influence in the Western Pacific. Russia will not ignore that example, and neither should we. Keeping our

strong maritime edge will demand continued awareness and pacing with RFN capabilities and capacity in both maritime and cyber domains.[61]

And these dynamics then translate into a demand signal for a larger and more capable maritime presence in the Atlantic Ocean and Mediterranean Sea in the mid-to long-term.[62] This is the language of arms races and great power rivalry at its clearest.

Indeed, Secretary of Defense Robert Gates now appears to be saying that we need missile defenses because of the Russian strategic nuclear force, and they will increase the significance of our nuclear deterrent forces. Certainly this is how Russia interprets his remarks, i.e., as a justification of its perception of prior hostility and confirmation of it.[63] This process obviously rekindles the possibility of a nuclear arms race, especially as Russia cannot conceive of America as anything other than an enemy.[64] Even if Russian diplomats say that Russo-American relations are better than what the media claims them to be, their own actions and those of other high-ranking officials belie this fact and point to a high degree of tension in the relationship.[65] And this remains the case even though President Dmitri Medvedev professes a hope for the continuation of the arms control and missile defense dialog with the next administration.[66] Certainly the recent foreign policy concept published in June 2008 reeks with hostility to U.S. policy.[67] Likewise, Medvedev's concept for European security, first outlined in a major speech in Berlin in June 2008 openly aims to reduce, if not extrude, U.S. influence in Europe.[68] Thus despite the self-evidently ludicrous charges that missile defenses in Poland and the Czech Republic represent a threat to Russia or that they are being emplaced because we regard Russian missiles as a threat to America (even though these defenses cannot intercept Russian missiles) or that bombers in Cuba somehow respond to NATO enlargement, clearly government pressure is forcing otherwise quite level-headed analysts like Dmitri Trenin of the Carnegie Endowment to adopt such arguments in public.[69] Therefore a virtual unanimity on the extent of the American threat is being enforced upon Russian opinion.

At the same time, such statements and trends also demonstrate the utter failure of American efforts to persuade Russia that it means to downgrade the role of nuclear weapons and presume its strategic policies towards Moscow on the basis of friendship, not hostility. On the one hand, the Bush administration argues that it has explicitly attempted to marginalize the use of nuclear weapons in American military strategy in its 2002 nuclear posture review (NPR).[70] Nonetheless, the administration's efforts to convince outside observers that their charges concerning the Nuclear Posture Review and subsequent policy that Washington relies excessively on nuclear forces; that the United States is either not reducing nuclear forces or doing so fast enough; that the United States is building new and more dangerous nuclear weapons; that the United States is lowering the threshold for nuclear weapons use by emphasizing preemption; and that these alleged failures and the supposed failure to sign new arms control treaties are encouraging proliferation are myths, fail to convince either domestic or foreign audiences that those charges have any foundation.[71] Instead, as Arbatov suggests above, for some time every existing and potential nuclear power, including Russia and America, has been moving to operationalize its nuclear weapons, assert a broader range of missions for them, and develop credible first and second-strike capabilities despite Russo-American reductions in strategic nuclear weapons.[72] This failure on the administration's part can be seen in Ambassador Brooks' statement above, for he was saying that we do not see Russia as an enemy with whom long cumbersome agreements based on mutual suspicion are necessary and pointed to numerous instances of agreements with Russia on issues of disarmament and proliferation.[73] Yet all this was of no avail and has failed to persuade Moscow of the truth of the administration's previous assertion of an end to mutual hostility.

This failure to persuade foreign audiences of our rectitude is directly traceable to the Bush administration's misguided strategic unilateralism that has only led to further nuclearization as in North Korea and potentially Iran, growing mistrust among allies and rivals alike, and a diminution of America's effective capabilities for projecting power in defense of its interests abroad. Obviously a new policy and a new strategy are needed. In the strategic and arms control areas, this failure is reflected not just in the invasion of Iraq and the disregard for many powers' opinions and interests, but in the fundamental tenets of the policy formulated and devised by President Bush and then Secretary of Defense Donald Rumsfeld in 2001-06. This policy clearly divorced force acquisitions and deployments from any concept of strategic and political realities relating to ties with major nuclear and military powers like Russia and China. It assumed they would go along with what seemingly is a transparent sign of American correctness, virtue, and attestations of friendship, but without any American reciprocity based on heeding their interests. This is not just a question of Iraq, it certainly applies to missile defenses and the withdrawal from the ABM treaty that Putin characterized as a mistake but to which he replied by also urging a new legal-political definition of strategic stability, i.e., a codified American strategic-political relationship with Russia. As Russian analyst Alexander Savelyev writes,

> It was obvious that the United States, for whatever reasons, ignored the Russian direct references to the importance of the strategic stability issue. The U.S. Administration just welcomed the part of Putin's statement about "no threat to the national security of the Russian Federation" and paid no attention to what Russia understood under such a threat. To my view, if we could speak of an American mistake, it was not the decision to withdraw from the ABM Treaty, but to completely ignore the principles which must create the basis for strategic relations with Russia after the Cold War; as well as the inability of the United States to present something instead of the "strategic stability" principle for the discussions and probable acceptance by the two states. And it was not enough to put forward standard ideas of "mutual interests and cooperation." The main problem and the task were to prove that the "strategic stability" principle must go, together with the Cold War and U.S.-Soviet confrontation. Since it has not been done, "strategic stability" continued to play a role of a "mine," which sooner or later could deeply worsen or even undermine U.S.-Russian strategic relations.[74]

Savelyev's critique parallels that of U.S. expert Dennis Gormley. Gormley observes that arms control theory and practices were predicated on mutual transparency. Neither the 2001 Nuclear Posture Review (NPR) nor the emphasis on missile defenses "was launched with any degree of reassuring candor and openness in mind." Although the NPR claimed Russia was not a threat and did not figure in our primary targeting plans, there was no awareness that revolutionary turns to depending on strategic strikes with conventional ABM atop nuclear launchers or nuclear warfighting strategies would affect Russian calculations about arms control or the proliferation of ballistic and cruise missiles abroad. "On global missile defenses, Russia and China were told not to fear limited American defenses. But the opaque nature of U.S. missile defense development—consisting of open-end system architecture and periodic block deployments—engenders strategic uncertainty rather than stabilizing transparency."[75] Hence the demand for exactly such a strategic stability dialogue based on deterrence called for by Lavrov above.

Therefore we could build missile defenses while remaining in a deterrent posture vis-a-vis Moscow and Beijing, militarize space, invade Iraq unilaterally and thus disregard the UN, enlarge NATO, and withdraw from arms control treaties, while expecting them to accept at face value protestations either of friendship or just simply accept that we are the strongest power who can do as it pleases. The uniquely anti-strategic thrust of a defense policy divorced from any realistic calculation of outstanding political realities is now exacting its demand for payment as a weakened America confronts the many bills it has incurred with fewer means of paying them and not just in economics.

Even if one is skeptical of arms control and deterrence as methods of preserving the peace, we must remember that other powers are wedded to these concepts, and their needs must be addressed. Furthermore, even arms control, pace Colin Gray, only succeeds if the problem for which it is invented is overcome, i.e., political and strategic rivalry among nuclear or major powers. Disregard or even merely perceived disregard for those powers' interests and concerns can only exacerbate the conditions that make meaningful arms control agreements harder to achieve.[76] Arms control negotiations with Russia have long since been proven to achieve the following goals: reinforcement of political understanding and dialogue, if not partnership, with Russia; greater allied cohesion and confidence in U.S. policy; downward pressure on proliferators as the nuclear powers are seen to be implementing the clauses of the Nonproliferation Treaty (NPT) calling for disarmament; and, most importantly, a general lowering of the likelihood of major power crisis or war that could escalate to the nuclear level. Failure to move forward on arms control, therefore, has an equal and opposite effect. And the present lack of progress on that agenda is reflected in heightened East-West tensions, diminished allied cohesion, as well as growing missile if not nuclear proliferation.[77]

The missile defense issue reflects many of these problems. According to F. Stephen Larrabee of the Rand Corporation,

> The Bush administration viewed the issue of missile defenses in Europe mainly as a technological issue, not a strategic one. Thus nobody anticipated public reactions or those of other governments to it. The plans for deploying a third site in Europe were drawn up by the Pentagon with little coordination with the State Department or National Security Council.[78]

Consequently, Poland and the Czech Republic were unable to respond to critics or answer questions in a timely manner. Not enough attention was paid either to public opinion in these countries or their domestic politics, and did not take into account the impact of this issue on the question of its relationship to European security. Thus we left out large areas of Europe that might need protection from Iranian missiles, e.g., Turkey or the NATO alliance as a whole. The technology for these defenses has also been plagued by unresolved questions and test failures. And this assessment does not even take into account the Russian objections, which apparently were not sufficiently foreseen.[79]

Should we persist along the lines of unthinking unilateralism here and ingrained hostility and suspicion in Russia, the results are already clear and present. Indeed, the best available studies of American nuclear policies, including modernization of those weapons, highlight the fact that these policies, including the introduction into practice of new concepts like dissuasion and preemptive, if not preventive war, could, if they have not already done so, develop into perceived *potential threats* to Russia in the near future.[80] Oddly enough, though, these potential threats are hardly ever mentioned in Russian commentary, which suggests the domestic and other factors that we pointed to are really the main drivers of national security thinking. To give one example, although the United States has upgraded its naval and other strategic forces and is gradually shifting them to the Pacific Ocean largely to meet potential North Korean or Chinese contingencies, these deployments also threaten Russian forces.[81] But Moscow has said little or nothing about these forces.

A second, equally negative possible outcome is that American policymakers will come to perceive Russia not just as a recalcitrant independent actor that does not want to cooperate with America, but as a potential or even active threat in its own right. This was already the case well before the Georgian war and had much to do with the progressive stifling of liberalism and democracy in Putin's Russia. Thus in 2007 Senator Joseph Biden (D-DE), long before he became Senator Obama's running mate, cited Russia as one of the three biggest threats facing America, precisely for that reason of stifling democracy.[82] Subsequent developments can only have further reinforced this perception and not only among Democrats. As this potential inheres primarily in Russia's nuclear capability, the developments cited here are already creating a climate among government circles (even before the war with Georgia) in which Russia can quickly come to be seen as a potential military threat due to its political differences with America. The Navy's recent musings along with those of Secretary Gates are mentioned above. In another example, the 2006 Report of the Defense Science Board on Nuclear Capabilities stated openly that nuclear reductions agreed to in the Moscow treaty of 2002 and recommended in the *Nuclear Posture Review* of 2001 pointed to a new and benign strategic relationship with Russia after the end of the Cold War and the desire to forge a new bilateral strategic relationship that no longer was based on the principles of Mutual Assured Destruction (MAD).

Today, the Report observes, that presumption of a new benign strategic relationship with Russia is increasingly open to doubt. This is because "Although United States relations with Russia are considered relatively benign at the moment (December 2006), Russia retains the capacity to destroy the United States in 30 minutes or less." Moreover, its reliance on nuclear weapons to compensate for a weakened conventional military has led it to emphasize nuclear weapons for purposes of maintaining superpower status, deterrence, and potentially warfighting. Russia's regression from democracy and rivalry with America over Iraq, Iran, and Central Asia (other issues may well be added since then to the mix — author) suggest that since the assessment of 2003, nothing had changed since 2001 to justify revising the NPR's presumption of a benign strategic relationship with Russia, needs to be revised.[83] Therefore the Report recommends the creation of a permanently standing assessment Red Team "to continuously assess the range of emerging and plausible nuclear capabilities that can threaten the United States and its allies and friends with potentially catastrophic consequences."[84] This team would monitor Russian, Chinese, and North Korean developments because,

> Despite the desire for improved relations with Russia, the direction, scope, and pace of the evolution of U.S. capabilities must be based on a realistic recognition that the United States and Russia are not yet the reliable, trusted friends needed for the United States to depart from a commitment to a robust nuclear deterrent. Intentions can change overnight; capabilities cannot.[85]

Other examples of a growing wariness about Russian intentions can also be cited.[86] Several recent articles have argued that Russia and China are modernizing their nuclear arsenals while ours is decaying, and that this trend could lead to the most portentous of strategic reversals across the globe for the United States unless it arrests the drift and starts to modernize its weapons as well. They postulate an unending scenario of fundamental international rivalry and hostility, not unlike that postulated by Russian analysts who therefore advocate both permanent deterrence and modernization.[87] Among these authors, Bradley Thayer and Thomas Skypek conclude that,

However, the reality is that there are no "time-outs" in international politics. The United States does not get to stop the clock in the realm of competition in strategic nuclear arms. All other nuclear countries are modernizing while the United States is not. If the United States ignores its lead in strategic systems, the lead will go away, and then recapturing it will be significantly more difficult due to the loss of infrastructure and knowledge.[88]

Thus there is a real danger that these perceptions can grow on both sides into self-fulfilling threat perceptions that will drive conventional and nuclear defense acquisitions and foreign policy decisions as well until they influence formal doctrinal and strategic pronouncements. Some Russian military observers have already openly postulated that Russia and America (or NATO) are still enemies. For example, Colonel Anatoly Tsyganok, a noted military commentator, speaking about the increase in large-scale and regular Russian military exercises, observed that apart from the need to conduct such exercises as part of the Army's regular routine, they are necessary to respond to American deployments in places like Hungary and Bulgaria. Both sides, he says, remain enemies and these exercises are hardly anti-terrorist ones but rather something else (i.e., he hints at their being intended to be anti-NATO).[89] Certainly and similarly, the so-called "Ivanov doctrine" of 2003 formalized in a Russian white paper that did not name NATO was oriented nonetheless to the primacy of a NATO/American threat.[90] And, as noted above, the new doctrine already is known to cast the United States and NATO as enemy number one.[91]

Nevertheless, for such threats to be actualized, the political climate between Moscow and Washington would have to decline still further. Consequently, while we should not rush to restore the Cold War, the present trends on both sides are disturbing and destabilizing, not only for what they mean to each other but also because of their impact on regional security throughout Eurasia and how they affect the calculations of other nuclear states or states that seek nuclear weapons like Iran and North Korea. In other words, these tensions cannot be confined to discussions of bilateral strategy and politics but deeply impinge upon the problems of regional security, global proliferation, and deterrence.

In the context of charges raised in 2006 that the United States has been striving for and now attained a usable first-strike nuclear capability against Russian forces—an argument that ignited a firestorm of polemics in Russia—such interactive Russian and American deployments of both conventional and nuclear forces do, in fact, raise the prospect of real as opposed to notional threats of an arms race where Washington seems to move for a supposed first-strike capability in both Russian and Western strategic analyses.[92] Thus David McDonough's analysis of U.S. nuclear deployments in the Pacific Ocean states that,

> The increased deployment of hard-target kill weapons in the Pacific could only aggravate Russian concerns over the survivability of its own nuclear arsenal. These silo-busters would be ideal to destroy the few hundred ICBM silos and Russia's infamously hardened command-and-control facilities as well as help reduce any warning time for Russian strategic forces, given their possible deployment and depressed trajectory. This is critical for a decapitation mission, due to the highly centralized command-and-control structure of the Russian posture, as well as to pre-empt any possible retaliation from the most on-alert Russian strategic forces. The Pacific also has a unique feature in that it is an area where gaps in Russian early-warning radar and the continued deterioration of its early-warning satellite coverage have made it effectively blind to any attack from this

theatre. This open-attack corridor would make any increase in Pacific-deployed SLBMs appear especially threatening.[93]

Similarly, already in 2003 when the first reports of the Pentagon's interest in new low-yield and bunker busting nuclear weapons became public, Russian analysts warned that even if such programs were merely in a research stage they would add to the hostile drift of Russo-American relations.[94] Events since then have only confirmed this assessment and their warning. Meanwhile, this trend continues towards increasing Russian reliance upon nuclear weapons against a perceived growing American threat. This threat perception and reliance upon nuclear weapons takes place despite American assertions that charges of excessive reliance on nuclear forces; that the United States is either not reducing nuclear forces or doing so fast enough; that the United States is building new and more dangerous nuclear weapons; that the United States is lowering the threshold for nuclear weapons use by emphasizing preemption; and that these alleged failures and the supposed failure to sign new arms control treaties are encouraging proliferation are myths.[95] So if we may paraphrase a famous movie line, "What we have here is a failure to communicate," while both sides appear to be sinking deeper into their self-justifying perceptions.

RUSSIA'S NEWLY ANNOUNCED POSITIONS

Fortunately the advent of new presidents in both Russia and America opens up possibilities for reversing the apparent stalemate in bilateral arms control despite the frigidity in relations generated by the war in Georgia. As candidates, Senators John McCain and Barack Obama appeared to share the traditional view that the centerpiece of our relations with Russia is arms control and have both supported the idea of negotiating a new START with Russia. This suggests a broad consensus in the Senate and House.[96] Obama, according to his website, goes further and says that he will:

> stop the development of new nuclear weapons; work with Russia to take U.S. and Russian ballistic missiles off hair trigger alert; seek dramatic reductions in U.S. and Russia stockpiles of nuclear weapons and material; and set a goal to expand the U.S.-Russian ban on intermediate range missiles so that the agreement is global.[97]

Obama also told Polish Prime Minister Donald Tusk that he supports the agreement with American missile defenses on condition that he is certain that it is not aimed against Russia. And Senator McCain was briefed by Warsaw that the missile defense network has nothing to do with Russia.[98]

Thus, based on their campaign rhetoric, both candidates accepted the Russian idea, rejected by the Bush administration, that this treaty should repeat or even amplify the extensive verification protocols of START 1 and 2 based on Lavrov's statement above. They are also close to Moscow's posture as regards the INF Treaty, i.e., globalizing the treaty. They do differ on missile defenses in Central and Eastern Europe with McCain supporting them and Obama being more critical, as noted above.[99] And this should suggest positive opportunities for progress with both Moscow and in the Senate which must ratify treaties.

The visible mutual hostility between the two powers and the attendant rising suspicion of their aims all but necessitates such an approach rather than the fatuous pronouncement that since we are not enemies, we can build what we like and so can you, that characterized the Bush administration's approach. Unfortunately, as the events of the past decade show, the Russian view is more realistic about world politics although much more backward-looking and negative. Still, despite its shortcomings, as we have said above, it cannot be ignored, disregarded, or simply overridden by unilateral action on our part.

However, again, and fortunately for us, we have a means of determining what it is that Russia wants from the United States with regard to arms control. Russia has just formally restated its position on all the outstanding arms control issues in its July 2008 Concept of Foreign Policy, and an examination of those positions allows us to see what drives Moscow and what opportunities there are for the next administration to advance U.S. interests and possibly global order interests as well, while at the same time engaging with Russia in a serious fashion.[100] Here it should also be noted that many, though perhaps not all, of the Foreign Policy concept's positions have been called for in earlier Russian statements, but those did not have the force of formal state documents like this paper.

First of all, Russia here calls once again for a strategic partnership with the United States. Thus the concept states that "Russia is building relations with the U.S. with consideration not only of their huge potential for mutually beneficial bilateral trade-economic, scientific-technological cooperation, but also their key effect on the state of global strategic stability and the international situation as a whole."[101]

Therefore all of the following proposals regarding arms control (and everything else for that matter) are conceived of in terms of addressing a changed global balance. Russia, which here sees itself as a major architect who is contributing to a new or developing world order, has broadened the concept of strategic stability to go beyond the erstwhile superpower relationship to encompass new actors and new regional balances. Those new actors are itself and China, India, perhaps Brazil, and Iran. In other words, Russia, even before President Medvedev claimed an undefined sphere of influence in August 2008, was announcing its determination to play in multiple regional balances as an equal to the United States and to restrain its capability for action, especially unilateral action, in areas not contiguous to Russia or the CIS.[102] This is a cardinal point that we should not lose sight of in our overall analysis of this concept. In this light, Russia calls for a genuine strategic partnership based on overcoming past barriers and confronting real threats and most of all, a partnership based on this endless quest for equal status with America.[103] Accordingly, Russia seeks new agreements in disarmament, arms control, to preserve the continuity of the process, agreements on trust and transparency regarding space and missile defenses, and a host of other issues like safe nuclear energy, proliferation, etc.

Asserting its probity as a consistent upholder and fulfiller of all existing arms control and disarmament treaties, Russia advocates the following positions regarding that agenda.

- Russia wants to negotiate with all nuclear powers (the United States, Britain, France, China) a treaty reducing strategic offensive arms (ICBMs, submarine launched ballistic missiles (SLBMs), heavy bombers, and the warheads placed on them to a minimum level sufficient for maintaining strategic stability.

- Moscow (like Beijing) speaks out against allowing the deployment of weapons in space, in favor of a system of "collective response" to missile threats on an equal basis, and against unilateral actions in the fields of missile defenses.

- Russia here argues that strategic stability can no longer be a concern solely of Russia and America. Therefore, the discussion must be opened up to all the major powers, primarily nuclear ones who are interested in joint action to preserve security. Specifically Moscow is also calling for globalizing the 1987 INF Treaty, which is to expire in 2009.

- Russia also opposed the development and deployment of what it calls destabilizing arms: new types of weapons, low capacity nuclear charges (which ironically it too is working on), ICBMs with conventional warheads, and strategic missile defenses.

- Russia professes to strengthen regional stability in Europe by taking part in the limitation and reduction of conventional forces, and the application of measures to enhance military trust on the basis of all the parties' equal security.[104]

Beyond these formal appeals, according to Dmitri Trenin of the Carnegie Endowment's Moscow office, Russia would also ideally like to negotiate a theater missile defense system to protect against missile threats to Europe from the Middle East (which is strange since Moscow still denies that such threats exist) that would replace the U.S. missile defenses in Poland and the Czech Republic. Moscow also, according to Trenin, would "welcome U.S. ratification of the Comprehensive Nuclear Test Ban Treaty, accession to the Fissile Materials Cut-off Treaty, and a pledge not to weaponize outer space."[105]

ANALYZING RUSSIAN PROPOSALS

The CFE Treaty.

To determine whether or not there are opportunities for the new U.S. administration to pursue mutually beneficial arms control agreements (be they conventional, nuclear, missile defense, or space weapons) with Russia, we must analyze what these proposals really mean, what lies behind them, and what purposes other than traditional propaganda gains they serve. Dismissing them simply as the same old propaganda, which these proposals may appear to be, gains nothing for us. That posture only impedes the realization of potential openings for an enhanced strategic dialogue with Moscow and other tangible strategic gains for us and possibly our allies. Furthermore, if we are to avoid falling into the trap described by Savelyev above, we need to clarify our understanding of Russia's positions so that we can present a meaningful reply to them that creates an intellectual and political basis for a new and enduring (because of its legitimacy) strategic order.

First of all, the foreign policy concept is as much a propaganda document as it is a formal policy statement. It represents an attempt to have others see Russia and its foreign policy as the Kremlin wishes them to be seen. Superficially, one might think that the concept exudes self-confidence with its numerous referrals to Russia's recovery and its important place as an architect of the developing world order.[106] But while every observer has commented on the newfound Russian aggressiveness and truculence of its foreign policy, in this concept, the lady doth protest too much. Constant references to the demand for equal security and to Russia's return to great power status betray instead an inner sense of weakness and even illegitimacy. States that are respected do not have to demand it, the demand signifying that Russia is acutely aware that it is not respected or equal to the United States. The reasons for this disrespect transcend this monograph, but they are clearly rooted in Russia's foreign policy behavior. Danish General Michael Clemmesen, the Commandant of the Baltic Defense College, writes in his blog analyzing the cyber-attacks in Estonia of April-May 2007 that,

> The attitude of Russia to the world and especially to its neighbors is presently close to that of the great power attitudes of that earlier [pre-World War I—author] period. It is built on a demand for *"respect"* for the country because of its size. It is rooted in the geostrategic and geopolitical attitudes tainted with Social-Darwinism that dominated the conservative elites of all *other* major European states of the period. . . . The respect demanded from the small—and thus contemptible and ridiculous—states on the borders is similar in type to that demanded by a mafia *"capo."* Presently the focus is in Georgia and Estonia. (Italics in original)[107]

Robert Dalsjo of the Swedish Defense Research Agency (FOI) concurs in every detail, noting that Russia's concept of power is that it can kick around smaller states to intimidate them, much like gangsters in American movies.[108]

One reason for this disrespect is the habitual mendacity that was so prominent in Soviet policy and that seems to have carried over to Russian policy in its fallacious attacks upon U.S. policy. For example, as we are considering the concept's arms control posture let us revisit the CFE treaty issue. Here Russia professes to strengthen regional stability in Europe by taking part in the limitation and reduction of conventional forces and the application of measures to enhance military trust on the basis of all the parties' equal security. In this context, equal security for Russia apparently means that it should have security equal to that of the United States and all of Europe. The frequent calls for equal security not only betray insecurity about Russia's status but are ultimately indefinable. Hence they cannot be resolved by political means but by a form of psychotherapy beyond the capabilities of governments and their leaders. But this demand has a long-standing pedigree. Many analysts inside Russia also have either advocated or noted that Russia demands a position equal to that of the United States at the "presidium table" of world affairs.[109] Thus Sergei Rogov, the director of the Institute for the USA and Canada (ISKAN) and a prominent advisor to the Ministry of Foreign Affairs, argued in 1997 that to counter NATO's disdain for Russia's interests and status,

> The aims of Russian diplomacy should be as follows: First of all, Moscow should seek to preserve the special character of Russian-American relations. Washington should recognize the exceptional status of the Russian Federation in the formation of a new system of international relations, a role different from that which Germany, Japan, China, or any other center of power plays in the global arena.[110]

But these statements were made in 1997 when Russia was going bankrupt. Now that it has recovered economically it is hardly surprising that it should voice these demands for a superior status even more

44

insistently. What this shows, of course, is that apart from Russian insecurity, under both the best and worst of circumstances, Russian elites are gripped by the mystique of being a great power. Indeed, Russian political writings are replete with references to this concept that Russia must either be a great power (and at home, a centralized autocratic state) or nothing and perhaps break up into the appendage principalities of medieval Russia. For instance, in 1999 at a meeting of the Academy of Military Science on future war that Sergeyev attended (Akademiya Voyennoi Nauke [AVN]), its director, Retired General Makhmut A. Gareyev, one of Russia's leading thinkers and a former Deputy Chief of Staff, stated openly that,

> One of the most important unifying factors is the idea of Russia's rebirth as a great power, not a regional power (it is situated in several large regions of Eurasia) but a truly great power on a global scale. This is determined not by someone's desire, not just by possession of nuclear weapons or by size of territory, but by the historical traditions and objective needs in the development of the Russian society and state. Either Russia will be a strong, independent, and unified power, uniting all peoples, republics, krays, and oblasts in the Eurasian territory, or it will fall apart, generating numerous conflicts, and then the entire international community will be unable to manage the situation on a continent with such an abundance of weapons of mass destruction. In the opinion of the president of the AVN (i.e., Gareyev himself — author), there is no other alternative.[111]

Furthermore, in the context of the CFE negotiations, Russia is a revisionist power. Moscow's demand for a free hand with regard to military deployments within the territory covered by the CFE treaty, for example the right to take unilateral actions short of withdrawal and suspend its participation, something that no other signatory has demanded, typifies its quest for a free hand and for unequal status and security vis-à-vis its interlocutors.[112] Thus Russia wants to freeze the process of European integration and replace it with a regional bipolarity. Similarly, the continuing presence of Russian forces in Moldova and until 2007 in Georgia has held the West back from ratifying the CFE treaty. Moscow used this as a pretext to suspend its compliance with that treaty and to threaten to leave it altogether.[113] But Moscow will not leave Moldova, or so it says, until a political treaty recognizing its forces' right to stay there comes into being. Russia also has other ulterior objectives there. For example, it seeks a 20-year lease on a base there to perpetuate its intervention on behalf of a separatist and visibly criminalized Russian faction across the Dniester River.[114] By obstructing conflict resolution here and in Georgia, Russia demonstrates its interests in preventing the completion of a durable European security order as well as regional integration into NATO and the European Union (EU).

We can see the real meaning of Russia's rhetoric in the fact that it unilaterally suspended its observance of the treaty, a move that has no legal status. It did so citing a nonexistent military threat in which it itself does not believe since otherwise it would not have left the protection of the treaty. The suspension itself has no legal standing or status and amounts to nothing more than what Russia accuses America of doing. Its refusal to negotiate unless its terms are accepted first belies its rhetoric about equal security. In practice the Vienna conference of June 2007 called to negotiate Russia's charges went nowhere. At the conference, Russia sought, but with no success, to pressure the West into "modernizing" the treaty in its favor mixing together all the issues, the treaty, missile defenses in

Europe, and Kosovo as a precedent in order to gain on at least one issue. In this context, it advanced six points with regard to the treaty.

- The 1999 adapted treaty must be ratified and brought into force quickly or at least declared to be "temporarily" valid by June 1, 2008.
- The Baltic states must sign the ratified treaty or at least the temporarily validated treaty to fall under its restrictions. As one commentator noted, Moscow also insists they should "return to the CFE Treaty which they quit in 1991, implying that as part of the Soviet Union in 1990 they inherited and accepted the treaty at that time, thus they do not have the right as sovereign states not to accept it."[115]
- New group limits should be negotiated on NATO armaments and hardware to "compensate" Russia for NATO's acceptance of new members and American installations in Romania and Bulgaria. Those countries' deployments and/or numerical ceilings should be lowered.
- The CFE treaty's "flank limits on Russian force deployments in the North Caucasus and Russia's northwest should be removed" because Russia "cannot and will not fulfill the provisions of the obsolete treaty to the detriment of its security" on this point. Since Russia has exceeded the treaty limits in the North Caucasus for years using a treaty escape clause with full Western understanding, this point presumably applies mainly to its northwest flank where there are no security challenges at all. But it certainly shows that Russia wants a totally free hand in and around the CIS and at home even though all the other signatories have renounced that goal. At the time Moscow announced that if no agreement

is reached on these and other Russian demands, e.g., keeping its forces in Moldova and Gudauta, Russia threatened to suspend compliance — i.e., exempt itself from the treaty's inspection regime, information exchanges, and quantitative force challenges — or even withdraw from the treaty. And on July 14, 2007, it announced its suspension of compliance with the treaty for another 150 days even though there is no legal provision for doing so within the treaty.[116] It also expects that other signatories would refrain from actions that "would hamper the treaty's revitalization" during such a suspension even though it arrogates to itself a legal right that does not exist in the treaty text.[117]

Not surprisingly, Russia's demands went nowhere and in practice came down to seeking a trade-off with NATO at Moldova's expense. But here again Moscow failed to achieve anything, leaving the Moldovan situation a standoff.[118] These issues have considerable importance for both Moldova and the conflicts around Georgia. In Moldova's case, we must remember that the Russian military leadership believes that its Moldovan deployments are a factor for stability there.[119] At the same time, Kommersant correspondent Boris Volkonsky pointed out at that time that Russia's demands for flexibility with regard to its troop limits and movements on the flanks while others are turned down reveals a key point. If they are not held down and Russia is, that opens the way to a major shift in the regional balance of power. So, to avert this shift, Russia must either withdraw from Moldova and Gudauta to get Western ratification and forsake its previous policies or risk the alternative spelled out by Volkonsky. Specifically,

As Putin has repeatedly stated, recognition of the independence of Kosovo, that is, the recognition of the rights of a nation to self-determination over the principle of territorial integrity, opens the way to acknowledgement of other unrecognized states. The CFE is a stumbling block exactly for that. Limitations on flanking countries and the possibility of transferring quotas among member states creates the possibility of a radical shift in the military balance in Europe as a whole and in its most critical spots. If Bulgaria or Romania, which cannot even hypothetically be subject to Russian attack, transfer their quota to Moldova or Georgia, and Russia cannot respond by increasing its contingent because of the treaty, the likelihood of a forcible solution to the problems of Transnistria, Abkhazia, and South Ossetia in favor of Tbilisi and Chisinau increases tremendously. Moscow cannot allow that to take place. It would undermine confidence in the country's leadership at home and put an end to Russia's pretensions to rebirth as a great power or even leadership in the former Soviet Union. That means that Moscow is going to renounce the CFE sooner or later. Preparations for that are being stepped up. The day after the beginning of the Vienna conference, the member states of the Collective Security Treaty Organization, which includes Armenia, Belarus, Kazakhstan, Kyrgyzstan, Russia, Tajikistan, and Uzbekistan, issued a statement saying that the CFE does not meet the interests of stability in Europe, the treaty's viability and effectiveness have passed and its further existence is subject to question.[120]

Not only did suspension of the treaty open the way for the possible recognition of Abkhazia and South Ossetia as has happened since the war began. Close reading of this analysis shows how all the key motor forces of Russian foreign policy: the drive for great power status equal to NATO despite the realities on the ground, the drive for a free hand in the CIS, and the subordination of treaty compliance to those drives also come together in the context of the CFE treaty and these conflicts. Nor do Russia's potential dilemmas end here. Since Russian forces are now leaving Georgia except for Gudauta, Georgia can sharply increase its forces up to the CFE treaty's limits or substitute a third power's forces, e.g., America's or some other member of NATO. This would become a real possibility should Georgia join NATO and become subject to its rules. Given the Russian perception of Georgia as a state that is eager to employ provocative and even coercive means to recover its territories, this could, according to some Russian analysts, threaten Russian vital interests since Russia is a Caucasian power and the conflicts in the North Caucasus and Transcaucasia are closely related to each other. Therefore, for Moscow it is critical that NATO and all other noncontiguous third powers (i.e., America) keep out of the Caucasus (a demand that also means binding Georgia and NATO to the CFE treaty's provisions).[121]

The complexities of the situation do not end here for the future of the Russian base at Gudauta, which is nominally in Georgia but actually in Abkhazia, also raises difficult issues in conjunction with the CFE treaty's provisions. Moscow claimed that only 400 military personnel remain there, half of whom are retirees and dependents. It acknowledges the presence of several combat and transport helicopters and some other military vehicles and facilities there but refuses to allow inspections under the CFE treaty as Georgia demands. Moscow argues that it needs to support "peacekeeping" forces in Abkhazia and the other "frozen conflicts." And such forces' number is not limited by the treaty, which also does not account for "unaccounted-for treaty-limited equipment" (UTLE) possessed by separatists in Abkhazia, South Ossetia, and Transnistria, all or most of which they got from the Russian army. Finally, Moscow argues that it needs flexibility to deploy forces there to deal with terrorist insurgencies in Chechnya and the North Caucasus. Russia made such demands at Vienna to no avail.[122] Since the presence of unaccounted for weaponry which either belongs to or could be transferred to these separatist enclaves is a major factor for continued instability and potential violence in these conflicts, Moscow's refusal to allow inspections under the treaty shows that it remains in violation of its provisions even as it demands that the West ratify the treaty unconditionally.[123] As a result, today there is no movement towards resolving the differences and the CFE treaty appears to be headed for the casualty ward of the arms control hospital. Indeed, Russia is already building air bases near Ukraine and is now going to get bases in Abkhazia and South Ossetia.[124]

Even before the war with Georgia, efforts to resolve the CFE impasse were going nowhere. Russia, during the spring of 2008, continued to argue that there was no legal link between the Istanbul Organization for Security and Cooperation in Europe (OSCE) agreements of 1999 calling for withdrawal from bases in Moldova and Georgia and the adapted 1999 version of the CFE treaty signed at Istanbul. NATO offered Moscow a so-called "parallel actions package." This calls upon NATO members to begin the ratification process (which can take months), while Russia resumes its withdrawal from those bases. Once those withdrawals were completed or Russia reached a settlement with Georgia and Moldova, all NATO members would strive to complete ratification of the adapted CFE treaty. NATO also pledged that after that it would address the Baltic accession issue to get the Baltic States to join the adapted treaty and take account of Russian demands to abolish the treaty's flank limits for it while retaining them for its neighbors like Norway, Turkey, and Georgia. Since the war began, Russia's behavior has made it quite unlikely that anyone would consider acceding to its demands, especially as the treaty's original intent is to limit the conventional forces of both sides and reduce the kind of threats generated by this war. Meanwhile, Russia refuses to be inspected under the CFE treaty's terms and its overall behavior is undermining confidence and security in Europe.[125]

For these reasons, it is probably not unfair to paraphrase Zbigniew Brzezinski's remarks about détente being buried under the sands of the Ogaden in 1978 with the observation that the CFE treaty is apparently buried under the hills of South Ossetia. As a result, there are signs on both sides of rethinking the plausibility of conventional war scenarios in Europe. For example, General Roger Brady, Commander of U.S. Air Forces Europe (USAFE), wants to procure more F-22 jets to patrol European skies and augment American air power capabilities in Europe from the decreased levels that had taken place since 1991.[126] Similarly, Western ministers of defense are considering a program to create a rapid reaction force that could easily be deployed into nations being threatened by Russia.[127] Finally, not to be undone, Russia is spending a record amount of money on its military in 2009 partly to offset inflation, but also to enhance its armed forces' capability, particularly that of the air force. It will raise spending on procurements in 2009 by 70 billion rubles in 2009, 40 billion rubles in 2010, and 60 billion rubles in 2011.[128]

The INF Treaty.

Although the situation is different with regard to the nuclear arms control issues, again we must grasp Russian motivations. For example, the threat in the Foreign Policy Concept that if the INF treaty is not globalized Russia will withdraw from the treaty goes back to 2005. Much evidence suggests that various political forces in Russia, particularly in the military community, are urging withdrawal from those treaties, not least because of NATO enlargement towards the CIS and U.S. foreign and military policy in those areas. In March 2005, Defense Minister Sergei Ivanov raised the question of withdrawal from the INF Treaty with the Pentagon.[129] Subsequently Ivanov stated that the INF treaty was a mistake.[130] After that, Baluyevsky followed suit, threatening to pull out of the treaty unless Washington ceased its missile defense plans.[131] More recently, on February 13, 2008, Russia made public a draft treaty on implementing restrictions on intermediate and short-range ground-launched missiles to globalize the INF treaty, claiming to welcome suggestions from interested states. At the UN General Assembly (UNGA) meetings of September 2007, a majority of members supported the idea of such a globalization, and the United States backed the idea in a joint statement with Russia on October 25, 2007, urging interested parties to discuss global elimination of ground-launched ballistic and cruise missiles whose range goes from 500-5000Km. But Washington has not supported the draft treaty.[132]

As part of this debate, General Vladimir Vasilenko also raised the issue of withdrawal from the treaty after Ivanov did so in 2005, though it is difficult to see what Russia gains from withdrawal from that treaty.[133] Indeed, withdrawal from the INF treaty makes no sense unless one believes that Russia is genuinely and — more importantly — imminently threatened by NATO, or Iran and China, but most of all by U.S. superior conventional military power, and cannot meet or deter that threat except by returning to the classical Cold War strategy of holding Europe hostage to nuclear attack to deter Washington and NATO. Similarly, with regard to China and Iran, absent a missile defense the only applicable Russian strategy to counter their nuclear and missile buildups would be to use nuclear weapons to deter them, but this means admitting that these supposed partners of Russia actually constitute a growing threat to it. Consequently, Moscow dare not admit that the enemy of America is also its enemy lest its domestically based foreign and defense policy that postulates partnership with China and Iran be seen to be inherently contradictory and even dangerous.

Thus the Concept's call for such a globalization of the INF treaty represents precisely Russia's efforts to pretend that an allegedly growing but actually declining NATO/U.S. threat should be countered by a strategy that aims to reduce both Iran's and even more China's missile and nuclear capabilities to threaten Russia. Indeed, on several occasions President Putin raised the idea of jettisoning the treaty if it cannot be globalized and calling it a relic of the Cold War. But he also was quite explicit that Russia was concerned about countries like China, Iran, and Pakistan. Thus in October 2007, he told Secretary of State Rice and Secretary of Defense Gates that,

> We need other international participants to assume the same obligations which have been assumed by the Russian Federation and the US. If we are unable to attain

such a goal . . . it will be difficult for us to keep within the framework of the treaty in a situation where other countries do develop such weapons systems, and among those are countries in our near vicinity.[134]

Since it is by no means clear that Russia can or should reply to any such threat by producing Intermediate Range Ballistic Missiles (IRBMs), the desire to leave the INF treaty and reactivate missile production of IRBMs represents only the interests of the defense and defense industrial sectors, not necessarily Russia's state interest. For example, in 2005 Vasilenko, anticipating Baluyevsky, also stated that the nature and composition of any future U.S./NATO missile defense would determine the nature and number of future Russian missile forces and systems even though, admittedly, any such missile defense systems could only defend against a few missiles at a time. Therefore,

Russia should give priority to high-survivable mobile ground and naval missile systems when planning the development of the force in the near and far future. . . . The quality of the strategic nuclear forces of Russia will have to be significantly improved in terms of adding to their capability of penetrating [missile defense] barriers and increasing the survivability of combat elements and enhancing the properties of surveillance and control systems.[135]

Obviously such advocacy represents a transparent demand for new, vast, and probably unaffordable military programs similar to the demand for reactivating production of IRBMs regardless of consequences. But it also reflects the belief in the United States as enemy and the adherence to deterrence as the only available means of preventing an American strike on Russia (even a conventional one). But in that case, Russia's government and military are, as Nikolai Sokov suggested, thereby postulating an inherent East-West enmity that is only partially and incompletely buttressed by mutual deterrence.[136] That posture makes no sense in a strategic climate where virtually every Russian military leader repeatedly proclaimed then, as did Baluyevsky through 2006, that no plan for war with NATO is under consideration, and that the main threat to Russia is terrorism, not NATO and not America.[137] Yet, on the other hand, Russian calls for renouncing the treaty and Moscow's associated demands for military construction harmonize perfectly with the aforementioned presupposition of a preceding and ongoing adversarial relationship with the West. Even if a new doctrine is being written because of NATO's enlargement, Moscow cannot sustain a Cold War type of arms race in Europe, and everybody knows it. So, should Russia leave the treaty, its policy would default to the option of building new IRBMs and all three legs of its nuclear triad. At the same time, that posture also is an open sign to Beijing and Tehran of Russian suspicions concerning their ambitions and capabilities. So while Russian generals do not raise these issues unless told to do so, their demands reflect that Russian strategic policy has again fallen into a dead end presupposing hostility to both the West and the East without the means to address either problem sufficiently.

Thus it would appear, as it does to Secretary Gates, that the real threat facing Russia is the rise of neighboring states' short and medium-range missile capabilities, e.g., Iran and China.[138] This is a fine irony inasmuch as Russia was instrumental in providing the wherewithal for these states' military development. If Moscow withdrew from the INF treaty, that would allow NATO to station INF missiles in the Baltic and Poland as well as lead China and Iran to step up their production of intermediate range missiles. Furthermore, because it is by no means clear that Moscow could regenerate production for both intermediate and intercontinental ballistic missiles as their plant for such production systematically misses production goals, withdrawal from the treaty could actually further diminish Russian security, not enhance it.[139]

The efforts to withdraw from the INF and CFE treaties are also connected to Russian fears that Western military-political pressure will be used to consolidate post-Soviet states' membership in NATO and/or the EU or to compel democratizing reforms in Russia or elsewhere in the CIS where Moscow supports the reigning authoritarians. Since Russia cannot compete militarily with the United States, let alone NATO, it has also openly discussed using its strategic and/or tactical (or so-called nonstrategic) nuclear weapons in a first strike mode in the event of a threat by either of those parties against it or its interests in the CIS.[140] Sergei Ivanov, among others, has threatened once again to put missiles into Kaliningrad if NATO does not take up Russian complaints about these treaties.[141] In early August 2008, there was a flurry of reports that Russia might even put nuclear missiles into Belarus. While this has been denied, it does appear that the Russian leadership is contemplating putting conventional missiles and air bases in Belarus to strike at missile defenses in Europe.[142] This issue refuses to go away as a possible "asymmetric response to NATO enlargement and missile defenses."[143] But Moscow already did this in Kaliningrad when it placed nuclear missiles there in 2001 and created a scandal thereby. Still, this recurrent discussion indicates a continuing inclination in at least certain circles to conduct unilateral and even menacing political and strategic actions using Russian nuclear weapons.[144] For instance, Moscow long ago gratuitously extended its nuclear umbrella to the CIS, even though none of those states publicly invited it to do so. But a plan for such deployment of newly produced IRBMs could only truly be taken to its logical culmination if Moscow frees itself from these two treaties that are pillars of arms control and security in Europe and renounces its interest in the continuing stabilization of European security.

The negative result of that is, of course, that this outcome reignites an arms race in Europe that, as Putin and Company knows, Russia cannot afford and that is in nobody's interest. Ironically, Russia actually depends for its security on the restraints imposed by those treaties upon NATO's members, including Washington. Moreover, it depends on them for subsidies through the Comprehensive Threat Reduction program to gain control over its nuclear, biological, and chemical weapons arsenals. Without that funding, it is quite likely that the recent visible regeneration of the Russian armed forces would have been greatly impeded because at least some of those funds would have had to go to maintain or destroy decaying nuclear, biological, and chemical weapons. Russia also needs Western, and especially American, help against terrorism emanating from Afghanistan or Iranian and North Korean nuclearization and is still interested as recent agreements show, in curtailing those states or terrorists' access to these materials.[145] Furthermore, it is no less at risk from Iranian missiles than anyone else (except possibly Israel), given the two states' hidden rivalry in the Caspian basin. Thus it needs or at least should need to cooperate with the West on proliferation concerns too. Therefore these efforts to withdraw from the relevant treaties are quite misguided insofar as Russia's real interests are concerned, even though Moscow's legal right to withdraw from a treaty is incontestable.

Finally, the call to globalize the INF is quite likely to founder on Chinese refusal to give away its trump card vis-à-vis Taiwan, America, Japan, and Russia. Since Beijing can undoubtedly see through Moscow's ploy of proposing nonstarter gambits in arms control as a way of asserting its great power status, system-forming character, international responsibility, and hope of running with Beijing and hunting with America, it is unnecessary for America to reject this proposal. Indeed, since Senators McCain and Obama have called for it, we need to ensure that our acceptance of this is contingent upon bringing China and Iran, and possibly the Indian and Pakistani governments to the table in order to get some transparency and restraint upon China's exploding missile and nuclear programs, Iranian programs, and the arms race in the Subcontinent.[146] Even if it is unlikely that these Asian states will accept the proposal, it also is important for us to start moving to curb not only ballistic but also cruise missiles which are breaking out across all of Asia.[147] And America benefits politically by not being seen as a nuclear spoiler.

Given this context of likely Asian skepticism if not refusal of this proposal and the obvious strategic and political disadvantages to Russia of leaving the INF treaty, we still need to understand why Moscow is floating the proposal, apart from the benefit of looking statesmanlike with regard to arms control and of trying to restrain both the Atlantic Alliance and China at the same time through one proposal. Here we must look at the state of Russian force development plans. Clearly the many calls for withdrawing from the INF system now justify such an action as a response, however "asymmetrical," to NATO enlargement, the emplacement of missile defenses in Eastern Europe, and the general advance of NATO and American military capabilities closer to Russia. So although Russia has, as of October 2008, not yet devised a new defense doctrine to replace the 2000 doctrine, all the reports emanating from Moscow claim that the new doctrine postulates NATO and the United States as the main enemies. Furthermore, its writing was undertaken at least in part because, "the analysis of the situation on the global arena points to the increasing demand for forcible actions in the policies conducted by the leading countries."[148] And in view of the deficiencies of Russian defense industry and what Putin and Company perceive as the mounting and ever approaching set of nuclear and conventional threats confronting Russia, Putin called once again for a "a new strategy of building armed forces until 2020" to strengthen national security.[149]

In 2004 when these issues of NATO enlargement, missile defense, and perceived alterations in U.S. military strategy began to heat up in Russian military-political discourse, Putin and Ivanov began to announce the development of unparalleled nuclear missiles that could give an effective asymmetric response. It was widely assumed that Putin, Ivanov, and Baluyevsky had in mind the *Topol-M* or RS-24 land-based mobile ICBM and/or the *Bulava* SLBM. But this is also when Ivanov and some generals raised the issue of leaving the INF treaty, touching off a major discussion among military-political elites.[150]

Despite the possibility that Russia's wounded defense industry cannot produce both IRBMs and ICBMs in sufficient quantity if it left the INF treaty, it is unlikely that the Ministry of Defense (MOD) thought this was the case. Otherwise they would not have raised the issue and continued doing so since 2005. Neither would they be likely to raise the threat of leaving this treaty, even though it would clearly provoke both NATO and China to respond by building more missiles, unless they believed they had the same or even greater capability to produce them. Evidently that is the case, or at least so the Russian military believes. So if China, as may well be expected, or Iran, or some other power refuses the call for such restrictions on these missiles, Moscow may well be planning to resume production or even crash production of them.[151] These new missiles could embrace a number of different categories of missile. One of them, described in 2005, was the revival of the Skorost' IRBM originally developed after 1983 but which was cancelled after one test due to the INF treaty. It has a 2,500Km range and is deployable in 2 minutes from a combat ready position and 9 minutes from the traveling position. Arguably, the cost of deploying it and the more recent *Iskander-E* missile (a version of the missile for export abroad) is considerably less then the cost of the *Topol-M* system.[152]

The *Iskander* missile is even more interesting a proposition. Undoubtedly as the prospects for serial production and deployment of the *Iskander* family of missiles grows, with plans being announced to deploy five rocket or missile brigades of *Iskander-M* missiles by 2015 with the first beginning in 2007, and given its attributes described below, it is incompatible with the INF treaty, and the Russian military evidently prefers to scrap the treaty rather than the production line as it had to do with all of Russia's IRBMs in 1987.[153] Indeed, General Vladimir Zaritsky stated in 2007 that Russia might deploy the *Iskander* in Belarus if America installs missile defenses in Poland and the Czech Republic and increase their range to 500Km, thereby violating the INF treaty, probably antecedent to Russia's withdrawal from it.[154]

In 1999 President Yeltsin reportedly signed a decree operationalizing the *Iskander* missile system with nuclear warheads (not the export version though). Evidently it has the following capabilities: "precision accuracy of fire"; control throughout the flight path; broad range of effective warheads that could be mounted on it; availability of battle management automation and information support systems; integration into global satellite navigation systems; ability to engage hardened targets; increase in the number of engaged targets per unit of time; ability to penetrate air and missile defenses; and capability to engage moving targets. Thus it could challenge any missile defense system within range, which is estimated as being between 280Km in the export version and 500Km so that it comes in under the INF guidelines.[155] Because the *Iskander* can be both a ballistic missile that can maneuver along its trajectory and a cruise missile, a new designation for the version of it that is a cruise missile system is *Iskander-K* (*Krylataya* or cruise in Russian). Therefore it can penetrate or evade ballistic missile defenses.[156] Indeed, the *Iskander-E* and presumably other variants seem to be designed to defeat Western ballistic missile defense systems including theater missile defenses, particularly the *Patriot Advanced Capability* (PAC)-2/3 low to high altitude air defense system.[157] According to Nikolai Gushchin, chief and senior designer of the Machine Building Design Office, the *Iskander* missile complex is also meant for covert preparation and launching of effective missile strikes at particularly important small-scale targets.[158] These capabilities make it an effective regional deterrent, so it is not surprising that its deployment at Kaliningrad or in Belarus and the reported sale of the *Iskander-E* export version at 280Km range to Belarus are often rumored as a riposte to the U.S. missile defenses in Europe.[159]

> The R-500, a new cruise missile adapted for the *Iskander* launcher, is reportedly designed to fly a radar-evading trajectory with an accuracy of three meters. The missile system is said to be able to easily overcome air and missile defenses, while its range remains limited to 500 kilometers, still in accordance with the INF Treaty.[160]

In 2007 Russia test-launched the ground-launched version cruise missile from the *Iskander-M* transporter-erector-launcher, whose range could exceed the 500Km limit of the INF treaty.[161] Reportedly, deployment should begin in or by 2010 and by 2016 Russia intends to equip at least five missile brigades with the *Iskander–M* complex (or *Iskander-K*).[162] If one follows Moscow's various *Iskander* missiles carefully, it becomes clear that there are at least three missiles, the export version (*Iskander-E*) which conforms to both the restrictions of the INF Treaty and the rules of the Missile Technology Control Regime (MTCR); the *Iskander-M*, which is for domestic Russian use and is a ballistic missile that apparently conforms to the INF's terms; and the newly-tested nuclear-capable *Iskander-K*, which is a launcher system with a Land Attack Cruise Missile (LACM), the R-500 (NATO designation SS-26), that appears to be intended to confound missile defenses.[163]

If Moscow leaves the INF, it would seem that its leaders anticipate being able to begin serial production of these *Iskander* missiles, and possibly the *Skorost'* missile, to target not only missile defense sites, but a wide range of European targets more generally. For this reason, those forces calling for withdrawal from the INF treaty apparently think they can deal with what most observers believe would be the resumption of an arms and missile race in Europe. In other words, the purposes of Russian IRBM missiles in Europe would be to threaten both missile defenses and Europe, possibly hoping again to detach it from America. Given what we have noted of Moscow's commitment to deterrence and presupposition of conflict with America, this logic suggests that important elements of the Russian military and political elite that Russia can only have security in Europe by ensuring Europe's insecurity through missile and nuclear threats. Baker Spring of the Heritage Foundation has captured the logic of this position by referring to the INF treaty's provisions for withdrawal. Spring writes that,

> The treaty requires the Russians to identify what extraordinary events related to the subject of the treaty have jeopardized Russia's supreme interests so as to justify withdrawal. Both Putin and Baluyevsky have indicated that Russia will point to the prospective deployment of missile defense systems in Europe as the justification. If the Russians justify withdrawal on this basis, they will leave no doubt that Europe is the target of the new missiles, and they will have stated that any attempt by Europe to defend itself with non-threatening, purely defensive systems is an inherent threat to Russia. In short, Russia apparently feels that its supreme interests depend on having an unfettered means to attack Europe.[164]

In this connection we must also understand the strategic political utility for Moscow of retaining

64

nuclear weapons that can exercise threats or deterrence, as the case may be, in a regional context. First, it is already banal to suggest that Russia here, like other states, develops nuclear weapons to offset America's conventional superiority and deter it. But beyond that point we can say that,

> War serves both as an instrument of policy and as a determinant of the structure of the international system. It is war, or the threat of war which determines whether there is a balance of power or a particular state becomes dominant. Therefore, adequate military power is needed to prevent any state dominating the international system. WMD are thus viewed as a non-conventional means aimed at preserving both regional and global balances of power. . . . Relevant to this argument is the idea that WMD, especially nuclear weapons, are needed to prevent a state from the temptation to make a clandestine dash to sole nuclear possession or, in other words, to close off nuclear adventurism.[165]

Thus WMD are also necessary for redressing conventional, not just nuclear, imbalances in military capabilities. This reasoning explains Russia's determination to force America to a position of parity with or strategic stability with it.[166] Not only do these weapons deter American and other powers' military action, they enable proliferators or weaker nuclear powers like Russia to throw off the strategic and military constraints imposed upon them by such imbalances. For Russia, this means a free hand in the CIS and a status as a co-equal to America, allowing it to try and constrain American decisionmaking. Brad Roberts' 1995 observation still holds true, namely, that,

> A threat-derived assessment of the proliferation dynamic blinds people to the simple fact that the primary implication of proliferation is not military but

political. The primary immediate effect of the ongoing diffusion of the ability to make high-leverage weapons is the creation of a technically empowered tier of states that can, if they choose, build and use high-leverage military instruments. . . . The emergence of a tier of states technically capable of producing high-leverage weapons is unprecedented in international affairs. Its emergence is coterminous with the end of the Cold War. The intersection of these two processes constitutes the unique moment in world affairs today.[167]

Proliferators or nuclear states like China and Russia can then deter regional or intercontinental attacks either by denial or by threat of retaliation.[168] Given a multipolar world structure with little ideological rivalry among major powers, it is unlikely that they will go to war with each other. Rather, like Russia, they will strive for exclusive hegemony in their own "sphere of influence" and use nuclear instruments towards that end. However, wars may well break out between major powers and weaker "peripheral" states or between peripheral and semiperipheral states given their lack of domestic legitimacy, the absence of the means of crisis prevention, the visible absence of crisis management mechanisms, and their strategic calculation that asymmetric wars might give them the victory or respite they need.[169] Simultaneously,

The states of periphery and semiperiphery have far more opportunities for political maneuvering. Since war remains a political option, these states may find it convenient to exercise their military power as a means for achieving political objectives. Thus international crises may increase in number. This has two important implications for the use of WMD. First, they may be used deliberately to offer a decisive victory (or in Russia's case, to achieve "intra-war escalation control" — author[170]) to the striker, or for defensive purposes when imbalances in military capabilities are significant; and second, crises increase the possibilities of inadvertent or accidental wars involving WMD.[171]

Obviously nuclear proliferators or states that are expanding their nuclear arsenals like Russia can exercise a great influence upon world politics if they chose to defy the prevailing consensus and use their weapons not as defensive weapons, as has been commonly thought, but as offensive weapons to threaten other states and deter nuclear powers. Their decision to go either for cooperative security and strengthened international military-political norms of action, or for individual national "egotism" will critically affect world politics. For, as Roberts observes,

> But if they drift away from those efforts [to bring about more cooperative security], the consequences could be profound. At the very least, the effective functioning of inherited mechanisms of world order, such as the special responsibility of the "great powers" in the management of the interstate system, especially problems of armed aggression, under the aegis of collective security, could be significantly impaired. Armed with the ability to defeat an intervention, or impose substantial costs in blood or money on an intervening force or the populaces of the nations marshaling that force, the newly empowered tier could bring an end to collective security operations, undermine the credibility of alliance commitments by the great powers, [undermine guarantees of extended deterrence by them to threatened nations and states] extend alliances of their own, and perhaps make wars of aggression on their neighbors or their own people.[172]

However, these trends also represent the conventionalization of nuclear weapons and nuclear warfighting scenarios where the nuclear power in question visualizes nuclear weapons as being like any other weapon and hence usable for specific military scenarios. Certainly, this is the case for Russia. For example, in an otherwise unremarkable interview General Vladimir Boldyrev, Commander in Chief of Russia's Ground Troops, described the missions of Russia's tank troops as follows,

> Tank troops are employed primarily on main axes to deliver powerful splitting attacks against the enemy to a great depth. Having great resistance to damage-producing elements of weapons of mass destruction, high firepower, and high mobility and maneuverability, they are capable of exploiting the results of nuclear and fire strikes to the fullest and achieving assigned objectives of a battle or operation in a short time.[173]

Indeed, from Boldyrev's remarks, we may discern that he, and presumably his colleagues, fully expect both sides to use nuclear weapons as strike weapons in combat operations. This process of conventionalizing nuclear weapons, in and of itself, substantially lowers the threshold for nuclear use just as Moscow did in 1999. At that time Colonel General Vladimir Yakovlev, Commander in Chief (CINC) of Russia's nuclear forces, stated that: "Russia, for objective reasons, is forced to lower the threshold for using nuclear weapons, extend the nuclear deterrent to smaller-scale conflicts and openly warn potential opponents about this."[174]

Allowing Russia to wriggle out of the INF treaty would open the door not just to a heightened arms race in Europe but to intensified Russian efforts to control the CIS, maintain forces on a reduced threshold in a deterrent relationship with the West for possible use in smaller-scale contingencies in and around the CIS, stimulate an acceleration of the missile "contagion" already visible in Asia, strike at nonproliferation, and end the half-century or longer drift towards the "de-bellicization" of Europe. For all these reasons, the Obama administration should support the idea of globalizing the INF treaty only if China and Iran agree to it. Otherwise, it should resolutely communicate its intention to uphold the treaty and seek to persuade Moscow to do so as well. Since the demand for this treaty is due to the perception of a heightened Chinese and Iranian threat, facilitated in no small measure by Russian proliferation to those regimes, the U.S. Government, consistent with the overwhelming strategic desirability of impeding a Sino-Russian alliance, should not carry Russia's water for it against China. Indeed, while a discussion of Chinese missile programs and policies is not within the purview of this monograph, it seems extremely difficult to imagine that China will relinquish its trump cards in Asia for no discernible equivalent and tangible strategic gain simply to make life easier for Russia. On a smaller scale, the same holds true for Iran.

But even if China and/or Iran refuse to accept this proposal, we should still not support Russian efforts to withdraw from it although that is Moscow's legal right. The immense security gains from this treaty must not be frittered away, nor should we say to Moscow that we welcome the extension of its deterrent relationships based on mutual suspicion toward other rising powers across the globe. Arguably, the road to success lies in moving from relationships based on hostility as in deterrence that stimulate trends for offensive buildup or lowered thresholds of nuclear use to one based on defenses aiming to limit damages with a secondary role for deterrence. Were forces reduced to about

1,000-1,500 warheads on both sides, i.e., below the 2012 notional SORT levels of 1,700-2,200, both sides would have sufficient second strike capability to deter any threats, and they can build defenses (which as Israel and Japan show, work, at least against IRBMs) on a mutually transparent basis.[175] This kind of approach would override the Russian perception of the need to abandon the INF treaty and could also overcome the phony crisis worked up by Moscow over missile defenses in Europe.

Tactical Nuclear Missiles.

Tactical Nuclear Weapons (TNW, or in Russian parlance, Non-Strategic Nuclear Weapons [NSNW]) are another issue in the bilateral arms control agenda. Yet Russia's Foreign Policy Concept is silent about them. This means that Russia is not seeking American action on this point or to reduce its holdings unilaterally (except where physically necessary) although it would like to raise the issue of U.S. TNW in Europe as a propaganda point. In other words, it perceives no threat from residual American TNW based in Europe. Rather, it seeks American inaction and clearly would prefer not to discuss this issue, suggesting that Russia still or once again harbors the intention of deploying its TNW to counter NATO enlargement and missile defenses in Europe. In the context of this monograph's analysis of Russian policy postures and recommendations for the United States, this anomaly cries out for explanation. TNW have been and remain a contentious issue between the two states. One reason for this contentiousness is that it has been all but impossible to arrive at a satisfactory definition of what constitutes TNW, how they are distinguished from strategic nuclear weapons, and then how to verify that one or both sides has destroyed that capability.[176] Following the 2001 definition by Vladimir Ryabchenkov, Counselor of the Russian Ministry of Foreign Affairs, we will designate TNW or NSNW as a class of weapons designed to engage objects in the depth of enemy deployment up to 300Km to accomplish a tactical mission. Under certain conditions TNW may be involved in operational and/or strategic missions. Operational nuclear weapons are a class of weapons designed to engage in the operational depth of the enemy deployment a distance of up to 600Km. Occasionally they may be used to accomplish strategic missions, or in exceptional cases, tactical missions.[177]

The problems connected with TNW also include other issues in the U.S.-Russian arms control agenda, specifically research (which is taking place on both sides) into low-yield nuclear weapons, something that again alarms Moscow because it is another manifestation of what it sees as Washington's unending penchant for breaking through the shackles of strategic stability and forcing it into a technologically driven arms race that it cannot possibly win. Thus Russia apparently envisages TNW as a counter to the prospect of American low-yield nuclear weapons and has been conducting research on such weapons for years.[178] Furthermore, while Russian TNW do not threaten the United States but rather Europe, U.S. TNW based in Europe become strategic weapons for Russia.[179] And typically, anticipating a worst-case scenario, the General Staff and members of the government refuse to rule out the future deployment by NATO of these weapons and clearly would like to deploy them in Kaliningrad, Belarus, and at sea, presumably in the Baltic Sea.[180] Thus, recently Nikolai Patrushev, Head of Russia's Security Council, charged that NATO membership for

Georgia and Ukraine could lead to the stationing there by NATO of TNW that could then perform strategic missions and carry strategic threats against Russia.[181] The fact that such charges are utterly fantastic and at variance with international treaties and Ukraine's constitution outlawing foreign bases on its territory is of little consequence in this manufactured paranoia. More recent statements suggest, however, that TNW may not be deployed in Kaliningrad but in areas close to Poland, including possibly the Baltic Fleet, once U.S. air and missile defenses go up in Poland.[182] This suggests that Foreign Minister Bildt's claims about TNW and the Baltic Fleet may be well-grounded.[183] Certainly, by their own admission, Russian officials like to sidestep discussions of TNW, especially in areas like Kaliningrad Oblast, by bringing up U.S. TNW in Europe and claiming that NATO cannot answer why they are there (in fact, NATO allies want them as a visible symbol of the U.S. commitment to Europe).[184]

Meanwhile Russia is also apparently working on low-yield nuclear weapons, ostensibly against U.S. TNW, but also possibly for deployment on its own TNW. For example, Viktor Mikhailov resigned as minister of Atomic Energy in 1998 in part to oversee development of a new generation of low-yield nuclear weapons used not just to counter NATO enlargement, but also to "make limited nuclear strikes during localized conflicts possible, presumably using TNW."[185] More recently an American study observed that,

> Press accounts and statements by government officials also suggest that Russia is engaged in R&D [research and development] on fourth-generation nuclear weapons capabilities—for example, precision low-yield nuclear weapons (possibly with yields as low as a few tens of tons), clean nuclear weapons (including

earth penetrators and neutron weapons), and weapons tailored to create special effects (such as electromagnetic pulse). Press reports also refer to more advanced or even exotic research into weapons based on pure fusion and nuclear isomers. The degree of investment and technical progress in these areas is uncertain, at least based on open sources, although some analysts suggest such capabilities would be highly consistent with official Russian doctrine, which emphasizes the role of nuclear weapons in deterring and prevailing in a broad range of nuclear and non-nuclear contingencies. If, as Russian doctrine proclaims, a lower nuclear threshold is required to deter conflict even down to the local level, then acquiring more usable nuclear weapons that could deliver decisive effects with presumably manageable escalation risk would be a logical development.[186]

Similarly, in 2004 it was reported that Baluyevsky said that since America's doctrine mentions the necessity of "direct applications of nuclear low-power nuclear warheads at the battlefield, Russia won't be removing TNW from its military arsenals." Putin has also expressed concern that the possibilities of American use of low-yield nuclear weapons for regional conflicts involving non-nuclear states or of conventional missiles atop nuclear launchers could lower the threshold for use of nuclear weapons to a dangerous level.[187] Of course, he failed to mention that Russia's similar research into low-yield weapons could have the same result, a factor that makes low-yield and TNW equally dangerous.[188] Baluyevsky alluded to what makes these low-yield weapons dangerous for both sides in 2004 when he said that,

> The United States should be the first to raise the threshold for the use of nuclear weapons to the super-maximum level — If the nuclear weapons, which formerly were seen only as a political instrument of deterrence

become battlefield weapons, that will be not simply scary but super-scary. We will be compelled to modify the development of our own strategic nuclear forces depending on Washington's plans for the use of these weapons.[189]

Furthermore, while Russian TNW do not threaten the United States but rather Europe, U.S. TNW based in Europe become strategic weapons for Russia.[190] Meanwhile, Russian research into low-yield weapons continues.[191] According to Ivan Safranchuk, Putin's 1999 statement (when he was head of Russia's Security Council) that President Yeltsin had endorsed a blueprint for the development and use of nonstrategic nuclear weapons means that Russia will develop "a new generation of nuclear munitions with low-yield and super low-yield delivered to the target by strategic launchers."[192]

Because it is virtually impossible to create a data exchange and verification regime for TNW, it has proven impossible to fully allay suspicions on both sides concerning each other's deployments. These weapons today are only subject to 1991-92 Presidential Nuclear Initiatives (PNIs), unilateral and parallel statements by Presidents George H. W. Bush, Mikhail Gorbachev, and Boris Yeltsin. These presidents declared their intention to store or eliminate warheads for TNW and NSNW, including shipborne weapons, except for a share of air-based weapons. Thus the "regime" for them is informal, not legally binding, and has no transparency or verification measures. Even aggregate numbers on both sides are unknown.[193] Moscow has no intention of changing this, preferring unilateral action to cooperation, again raising suspicions concerning its ulterior motives for using these weapons. For example, in 2004 a defense official told the press that "If you want, take our word for it. If you don't want to, then don't. But we are not going to report back to anybody with figures in our hands about how many and what kind of specific tactical nuclear arms we have reduced."[194]

Therefore, most analysts accept these weapons' importance for Russia. As Pavel Podvig wrote in 2001,

> According to the view that almost all Russian military and security analysts share, the only practical way of dealing with a confrontation with the United States is to resort to nuclear weapons. The Russian military doctrine, adopted in April 2000, specifically reserves the right to use nuclear weapons in response to a full-scale non-nuclear aggression with the apparent goal of deterring it. The text of the doctrine does not say, perhaps intentionally, what kind of nuclear capabilities Russia might need to deter a conventional aggression, but the common understanding of the doctrinal language is that it means reliance on tactical nuclear weapons.[195]

Since then, not only have statements by people like Retired General Vladimir Belous, Senior Analyst at the Institute of International Relations and World Economics (IMEMO), openly referred to the use of TNW in deterrence mode against conventional aggression, Russian exercises in 2004 (Soyuznaya Bezopasnost' [Union Security]) involved the use of TNW against a sudden aggression of superior enemy forces. As a result, many Russian analysts have argued that the continued use or threat of use of TNW means that these weapons, which are seen as warfighting weapons much more than are ICBMs or SLBMs, will heighten the existing deterrence relationship between East and West and irretrievably poison their relations.[196] Gunnar Arbman and Charles Thornton of the Swedish Defense Research Agency similarly conclude that,

If possible, Russia may have further lowered its nuclear threshold, perhaps even compared to Soviet policy during the Cold War. The simple doctrinal statement that Russia will be a first user of nuclear weapons if its conventional forces are found to be inadequate in an armed conflict of some magnitude essentially guarantees early use of (T) NW's in a conflict with any sizable opponent, and all the more so if this opponent is equipped with more modern conventional arms than Russia.[197]

Unfortunately these warnings have been proven to be true. Both sides now utter public statements revealing their suspicions about each other's deployments. Thus Sergei Ivanov, as Defense Minister, claimed there was no reason for NATO to maintain TNW in Europe.[198] In 2006 Assistant Secretary of State for Arms Control Stephen Rademaker said that Russia had not fulfilled its side of the PNI. While America still had a relatively small number of TNW in Europe, the number had been cut 90 percent since 1991. But Russia has not seen fit to reciprocate. Analysts attributed this to the continuing desire to keep these weapons (as well as the *Iskander* missiles) in reserve as possible deterrents.[199] In fact, according to a Natural Resources Defense Council Report in 2005, America stored 480 nuclear weapons in Europe, more than twice what was believed to be the case. If this be true, it is no surprise why Moscow is not reciprocating even though Rademaker's claims about U.S. cuts represent official policy.[200]

Absent clarity from Moscow either in a new doctrine or policy statement, it is unclear whether the role of TNW is growing, though the pressure to withdraw from the INF and to retaliate against the emplacement of missile defenses in Europe suggests that this is the case. The *Iskander* in one of its many forms could be the centerpiece of a new generation of such weapons or other older versions may still be operable. While most of them are concentrated today in the Air Force, it appears that the Navy, as of 2003, is still lobbying for the return of NSNW to surface ships lest they not be able to contend with other foreign navies including the U.S. Navy.[201] Whatever decision Russia makes will undoubtedly be affected by U.S. policy, e.g., what we do with our missiles in Europe, missile defenses, and NATO enlargement.[202] But the utility of these weapons as seen from the Russian armed forces' perspective cannot be denied, so it is quite unlikely they will give them up without a reciprocal major arms control concession.

> The role of nonstrategic nuclear forces in Russian military doctrine and strategy has been important and a matter of some contention . . . Nonstrategic nuclear weapons have been discussed in a variety of contexts by Russian defense officials and commentators, including: (1) their role in negating or deterring possible attacks by opponents capable of attacking Russia with strategic conventional weapons based on information superiority (so-called Sixth-Generation Warfare); (2) their use for the purpose of avoiding military defeat in a conventional war while deescalating the conflict to Russian advantage; (3) their role in helping to preserve combat stability, or continuity of mission performance during enemy attacks, as a factor of equal or greater importance to survivability of nuclear forces.[203]

Accordingly, Russia sees TNW as one of the tiers of its deterrence structure, allowing it to deter or escalate, i.e., TNW give Russia more flexible options in crisis situations and even the possibility of controlling intrawar escalation.[204] By 2004 it was clear to Russia, based on the experience of exercises and due to mounting anger about NATO enlargement, that the first use of TNW in a European theater conflict was quite likely.[205] Consequently, Moscow's PNI statements consistently say it is gradually reducing the number of TNW by reporting percentages of implementation, not real numbers. But at the same time, these statements make clear that Moscow regards it as impossible to separate discussions of TNW from those of other armaments as Washington does.[206] Therefore Russia will only negotiate the reduction of TNW with America if Great Britain and France (if not others) are engaged because Russia needs TNW to contain aggression, particularly from its south, i.e., Iran and the Middle East. Russia claims to have withdrawn 60 percent of the air defense forces' TNW, 50 percent of the Air Force's TNW, 30 percent of the Navy's, and 100 percent of the Army's TNF. "But they will be there again, if necessary, and nobody should doubt it" according to Colonel General Vladimir Verkhovtsev, Chief of the 12th Main Directorate of the Ministry of Defense (responsible for nuclear weapons). Indeed, because the United States still has nuclear weapons in Europe, any reduction by Russia would negatively affect its security.[207]

Since American officials regard Moscow's demands for reciprocity and for tying these systems into larger negotiations as stalling devices, and moreover America's allies have made clear their desire to retain those weapons in Europe until and unless East-West relations improve, it is unlikely there will be progress on this issue and that apparently suits Moscow's preferences.[208] If the next administration is serious about moving toward a non-nuclear world, it might want to revisit this issue, but it cannot do so unless our NATO allies signal their willingness to reduce or even dispense with TNW and until the issue of missile defenses in Europe is resolved. If those defenses are further developed into a ramified network as Russia fears, then they could conceivably negate Russia's TNW. But such developments would only lead to further missile constructions and deployment as Moscow keeps threatening to do.[209]

In other words, Russia intends, as part of its deterrence policy, to keep America's allies hostage as shown by its threats of missile strikes against Poland, the Czech Republic, Ukraine, and now Western Europe for either hosting missile defenses systems or joining NATO. Failure to resolve TNW issues, like Russian projected deployment of missiles in Kaliningrad and Belarus, increasingly makes no political or strategic sense.[210] Instead, the next administration should soon try to find a way of negotiating away all TNW in Europe and call Moscow's bluff so that our allies are not held hostage to the revanchism and revisionism of the new Russian autocracy.

Indeed, sources across Central and Eastern Europe report a sense of fear among many sectors at being caught in the middle of an East-West struggle, especially as Russia is apparently building up air bases near Ukraine now that it has suspended participation in the CFE treaty.[211] Loose talk about deploying missiles or even nuclear weapons in Belarus or Kaliningrad, or near Poland also adds to tensions. Russia also is now apparently threatening Bulgaria, saying the building of a missile shield will undermine its relations with Russia.[212] Moscow has also threatened to target Georgia for missile strikes if it joins NATO.[213] It should be noted that if missile defense systems are installed in Poland and the Czech Republic, they will be more than 500Km away from the potential sites for the *Iskander* which means that essentially Moscow is threatening countervalue strikes on places like

Warsaw or withdrawal from the INF treaty followed by the building of weapons that could then target both these countries and the missile defense sites.[214] Therefore, only in the larger context of arms control will we and Moscow be able to address the issue of TNW. But until then, continued delay has its costs, as it only generates more pressure within the paranoid Russian military-political elite to develop TNW, low-yield nuclear weapons, and cruise missiles like the *Iskander-K*, given their belief that only if Europe is insecure and under threat from Russia, can Russia have security. On that basis, the retention of older systems, if not the construction of new TNW, appears to be a compelling military requirement for Moscow, which sees no reason to bargain them away for U.S. nuclear weapons in Europe, especially as it understands that the allies want them to stay. Until and unless there is progress on INF and missile defenses or a formal proposal to go to zero on both sides, this strategic requirement will probably remain for Moscow and can only be addressed in a larger framework of East-West relations. Inevitably, that retention and likely further development of Russian TNW will further poison ties with Europe and America and further underscore Moscow's belief that its security is contingent upon Europe's insecurity and intimidation.

Space Weapons.

The Bush administration's professed interest in weaponizing space, and in doing so not solely in conjunction with missile defenses, is profoundly troubling for Russia. Russian writers and officials fear that this program is another way in which the United States can break free of strategic stability and threaten not only Russia's nuclear weapons, but its C3I space systems including satellites and the ground-based infrastructure that supports them. After all, President Bush signed an order in October 2006 "tacitly asserting the U.S. right to space weapons and opposing the development of treaties or other measures restricting them."[215] Thus Russian analysts acknowledge the rising possibility that in future conflicts space will not only be militarized, i.e., used for military purposes, but also weaponized, particularly in a way that allows America to break free of the shackles Russia wants to fashion through strategic stability.[216] As Peter Rainov observes, Russian writings fully grasp the looming threat of space war. Thus,

> Space warfare is emerging as the most significant sphere of military operation[s] in any future major war due to its importance in reconnaissance, electronic, and information warfare. In the period up to 2020-30 Russian authors see it as an extension of other airspace operations. The expected future introduction of specific space offensive weaponry in addition to anti-satellite weapons, according to some experts, could transform all of space into two major theaters of strategic operations: the near space theater and the lunar theater.[217]

Because terrestrial and even submarine and space warfare are becoming increasingly integrated operationally, space capabilities to project power to the earth, sea, and underwater will become a decisive factor of war as well, further challenging backward Russia.[218] Consequently, we should not have been surprised that in September 2008 Russia announced that it would build a space defense system.[219]

Indeed, for all the boasting about asymmetric ripostes to American innovations, Russian leaders know and admit that their air and space defenses cannot defend against the threats they perceive from the United States, including not just missiles, but also space-based systems.[220] Commander in Chief of the Air Force General Alexander Zelin publicly stated that these particular threats to Russia are of the greatest significance while its air and space defenses are in critical condition. Therefore, by 2020 the entire country will be vulnerable to foreign air and space attack.[221] So much for the numerous boasts that Russia has the missiles that can nullify any missile defenses or that its defenses can detect and destroy any ICBM warheads.[222] Thus Baluyevsky, for example, warned that the planned U.S. deployment of missile defenses in Europe threatens not only Russia's deterrent, but also could lead to the deployment of missile defense space-strike systems that pose a special danger to global stability.[223] Certainly Russian officials see the weaponization of space, the integration of space and terrestrial capabilities, missile defenses, and the U.S. global strike strategy as a part of a systematic, comprehensive strategy to threaten Russia as Lavrov suggested above.[224]

Russia has responded in four ways to this threat. First, already by 2000, it was helping China to modernize and extend the range and precision of its ICBM and SLBM missiles and missile defense capability to threaten the continental United States, diversify and expand its arsenal, and counter foreign missile attacks in the event of conflict over Taiwan or elsewhere in Asia. This is only part of a much larger and still ongoing Chinese comprehensive modernization of military technologies that aims to give China the means to fight for informational and strategic superiority by striking the enemy's most critical targets first, even preemptively This strategy and target set could easily mandate space war and/or nuclear attacks.[225] There is no reason to believe that this assistance has been discontinued despite China's demonstration of an anti-satellite (ASAT) capability in 2007. Second, along with China, Russia has tabled a draft treaty at the UN Disarmament conference in Geneva, banning space weapons. It has no chance of going through, as Washington sees it for what it is, an attempt to impose a ban on its weapons and missile defenses in Europe. Such gambits might have some traction, since many states are alarmed at the prospect of an arms race in space, given China's visible capabilities there. But it is not likely to be anything more than a political and propaganda gesture.[226] Moscow and Beijing have been fighting the so-called "militarization of space" since at least 2002.[227]

But this draft treaty is particularly interesting. The current regime for space dates back to the 1967 Outer Space Treaty that forbids the deployment of WMD, military facilities, weapon testing, or maneuvers on the moon or other celestial bodies. But it does not ban conventional weapons. The Russo-Chinese draft, however, bans the deployment and testing of space weapons but not research, development, or production. As a recent assessment observes, even as China is reported to be aggressively developing anti-satellite weapons with the space and counterspace assets they omitted to ban from their draft treaty. "This huge lacuna runs the risk of allowing, even encouraging, the development of a potential counter-space 'breakout' capability — that is, a clandestine but untested anti-satellite (ASAT) system — while still remaining within the treaty's limits."[228]

Likewise, this draft is silent about terrestrially based systems, e.g., direct ascent, radio-frequency, and directed energy weapons that are the next wave of counter-space capabilities, especially for China, which is involved in both kinetic and nonkinetic counterspace programs.[229] There are other thorny issues related to verification of any such treaty. But it is clear from the foregoing that this draft is a tendentious and one-sided effort to cripple U.S. programs.

Third, Russia has announced its intention to retaliate if other nations deploy space weapons.[230] Indeed, since its analysts have already acknowledged the likely further militarization of space, a process to which it has contributed in the past, it really has no choice.[231] Indeed, it already is building a new Angara space rocket at the Plesetsk site in Arkhangelsk Oblast.[232] Alternatively, if Russia cannot develop its space-based forces sufficiently, some experts believe it can develop its ground-based counterspace (ASATs?) potential until it can cause the enemy unacceptable damage. This would include missiles with short active boost phase or maneuverable warheads.[233] Unfortunately for Moscow, its efforts to maintain even its reconnaissance and communications satellites in space, e.g., the Global Navigation system GLONASS, are faltering or failing to keep up, and it is unlikely that Russia will be able to place weapons in space worthy of being targeted. This evidently is true even if America does weaponize space because Russia's experience with ASAT capabilities has been disappointing. The benefit to Russia is that its forces' limited dependence upon space assets does not make its military overly vulnerable to attacks on those assets. Therefore, according to Pavel Podvig, it may counter any space weaponization with asymmetric means that should be relatively easy for it to accomplish. For example, he noted the discussion of emplacing missiles in Kaliningrad and Belarus and of the extension of the life of Multiple Independently Targetable Reentry Vehicles (MIRV) systems are rejoinders to the development of missile defenses in Europe. Such deployments, as noted above, are quite destabilizing for European security. But beyond that, as Podvig notes, the small likelihood of a Russian weapons system in space puts into question the desirability of our doing so to deal with Russia.[234] China, of course, may be a different story. Nonetheless, the next administration needs to take a hard look at the trends, benefits, and costs relating to the weaponization of space beyond existing conditions of the use of satellites and reconnaissance systems.

It may or may not turn out to be necessary and/or desirable to undertake such weaponization. But it should be clear that if we do, Russia will retaliate, either unilaterally to counter our actions and/or by drawing closer to China. Given the fact that any such alliance makes China the dominant partner against Russia's preferences, that is decidedly not in our, or for that matter, Russia's interest. Here it should be clear to us that China's capabilities threaten Russia's interests as much as they do ours. Second, we should consider the consequences if Russia is not really a useful target of future American weapons, of such an emplacement, as it could lead to a Russo-Chinese alliance.

Consequently, the danger is that this ideological-strategic rivalry will harden, leading to a polarized, bilateral, and hostile division of Asia into blocs based on a Sino-Russian bloc confronting a U.S. alliance system led by alliances with Japan, South Korea, and Australia. Some Western writers have already opined that Sino-Russian relations appear to be tending towards an anti-American alliance in both Northeast and Central Asia.[235] But more recently both Asian and Western writers have begun to argue that such a polarization in Asia could be taking shape. The shared interest of perceiving America as an ideological and geopolitical threat has also united Moscow and Beijing in a common cause.[236] Already in the 1990s, prominent analysts of world politics like Richard Betts and Robert Jervis, and then subsequent Central Intelligence Agency (CIA) studies, postulated that the greatest security threat to American interests would be a Russian-Chinese alliance.[237] Arguably, that is happening now and occurs under conditions of the energy crisis that magnifies Russia's importance to China beyond providing diplomatic support, cover for China's strategic rear, and arms sales.[238]

That alliance would encompass the following points of friction with Washington: strategic resistance to U.S. interests in Central and Northeast Asia, resistance to antiproliferation and pressures upon the regimes in Iran and North Korea, an energy alliance, an ideological counteroffensive against U.S. support for democratization abroad, and the rearming of both Russia and China, if not their proxies and allies, with a view towards conflict with America.[239] One South Korean columnist, Kim Yo'ng Hu'i, wrote in 2005 that,

China and Russia are reviving their past strategic partnership to face their strongest rival, the United States. A structure of strategic competition and confrontation between the United States and India on the one side, and Russia and China on the other is unfolding in the eastern half of the Eurasian continent including the Korean peninsula. Such a situation will definitely bring a huge wave of shock to the Korean peninsula, directly dealing with the strategic flexibility of U.S. forces in Korea. If China and Russia train their military forces together in the sea off the coast of China's Liaodong Peninsula, it will also have an effect on the 21st century strategic plan of Korea. We will now need to think of Northeast Asia on a much broader scale. The eastern half of Eurasia, including Central Asia, has to be included in our strategic plan for the future.[240]

Since then, Lyle Goldstein and Vitaly Kozyrev have similarly written that,

> If the Kremlin favors Beijing, the resulting Sino-Russian energy nexus—joining the world's fastest growing energy consumer with one of the world's fastest growing producers—would support China's growing claim to regional preeminence. From Beijing's point of view, this relationship would promise a relatively secure and stable foundation for one of history's most extraordinary economic transformations. At stake are energy reserves in eastern Russia that far exceed those in the entire Caspian basin. Moreover, according to Chinese strategists, robust Sino-Russian energy links would decrease the vulnerability of Beijing's sea lines of communication to forms of "external pressure" in case of a crisis concerning Taiwan or the South China Sea. From the standpoint of global politics, the formation of the Sino-Russian energy nexus would represent a strong consolidation of an emergent bipolar structure in East Asia, with one pole led by China (and including Russia) and one led by the United States (and including Japan).[241]

Russia's tie to China certainly expresses a deep strategic identity or congruence of interests on a host of issues from Korea to Central Asia and could have significant military implications. Those implications are not just due to Russian arms sales to China, which are clearly tied to an anti-American military scenario, most probably connected with Taiwan. They also include the possibility of joint military action in response to a regime crisis in the DPRK.[242]

MISSILE DEFENSES

As the foregoing analysis suggests, in our strategic nuclear dialogue with Moscow (and Beijing), we cannot lose sight of the fact that trends in force deployments and strategy simultaneously affect strategic-political developments in both Europe and Asia. If for no other reason, from Russia's perspective, U.S. technological and military advances across the spectrum of high-tech, precision-based conventional warfare, space, and nuclear weapons all threaten to unhinge the relationship of strategic stability, giving Washington what Russian leaders dread, i.e., a belief that they can use or threaten to use nuclear weapons to coerce Russia into surrender. Thus both the alleged and real threats posed by missile defenses, among other potential breakout systems, are not just military issues in nature but also political questions. The issues of the development of missile defenses in the Czech Republic and Poland, and around the Pacific rim, exemplify this fact even if the consequences and circumstances of these deployments differ in each region.

Precisely because analyses of this issue now focus on Europe at the expense of Asia, we will reverse that trend and deal with the impact of these defenses upon Russia in Asia, bearing in mind that we must factor China's nuclear capabilities into this equation along with the fact of North Korean proliferation. Moscow must protect against such contingencies that could emerge from China's growing nuclear and military capabilities as well as against the consequences of North Korean proliferation. Absent missile defenses and even sufficient conventional defenses against China, Russia must at all costs be friendly with China (though not necessarily an ally) even as it deters China with its nuclear capabilities. Consequently, Russia is steadily building up those nuclear capabilities in both the Pacific Fleet and its ICBMs. Likewise, in order to avoid being marginalized in regard to the Korean issue, it has restored a dialogue with Pyongyang and taken part in the six-party process to denuclearize the DPRK.

As McDonough showed above, U.S. force deployments in the Pacific theater definitely threaten Russian nuclear assets and infrastructure as well as its territory and conventional forces.[243] A second major Russian concern is the strengthening of the U.S.-Japan alliance in the twin forms of joint missile defenses and the apparent consolidation of a tripartite or possibly quadripartite alliance including Australia and South Korea, if not India. In that context, both Moscow and Beijing worry that North Korean nuclearization might lead Japan to build nuclear weapons. But beyond that, for both Russia and China, one of the most visible negative consequences of the DPRK's nuclear and missile tests has been the strengthened impetus it gave to U.S.-Japan cooperation on missile defense. The issue of missile defense in Asia had been in a kind of abeyance until the North Korean nuclear tests of 2006. These tests, taken in defiance of Chinese warnings against nuclearization and testing, intensified and accelerated U.S.-Japanese collaboration on missile defenses as the justification for them had now been incontrovertibly demonstrated. But such programs always entail checking China's nuclear capabilities and even, according to Beijing, threatening it with a first strike. Naturally those developments greatly annoy China.[244] Therefore China continues publicly to criticize U.S.-Japan collaboration on missile defenses.[245] Perhaps this issue was on Chinese President Hu Jintao's agenda in September 2007 when he called for greater Russo-Chinese cooperation in Asia-Pacific security.[246]

His remarks may have prompted Russia to act or speak out against these trends in Asia for Russia, having hitherto been publicly reticent to comment on this missile defense cooperation or to attack the U.S. alliance system in Asia, reacted quite strongly.[247] During Lavrov's visit to Japan in October 2007 and despite his strong pitch for Russo-Japanese economic cooperation, he publicly warned that Russia fears that this missile defense system represents an effort to ensure American military superiority and that the development and deployment of such systems could spur regional and global arms races. Lavrov also noted that Russia pays close attention to the U.S.-Japan alliance and was worried by the strengthening of the triangle comprising both these states and Australia.[248] He observed that "a closed format for military and political alliances" does not facilitate peace and "will not be able to increase mutual trust in the region," thereby triggering reactions contrary to the expectations of Washington, Tokyo, and Canberra.[249] More recently, at the 2008 annual Association of Southeast Asian Nations Regional Forum (ARF) in Singapore, Lavrov again inveighed against "narrow military alliances," claiming that Asian-Pacific security should be all-inclusive and indivisible, the work of all interested parties, not blocs. Any such activity must enhance strategic balance and take account of everyone's interests and be based on international law, i.e., the Security Council where Moscow has a veto.[250]

Lavrov's complaints show what happens when bilateral cooperation breaks down and, as a result of proliferation, overall regional tensions increase, in this case in Northeast Asia. Russia has responded to the U.S. missile defense program in both Europe and Asia by MIRVing its existing and older ICBMs, (that is, putting so called MIRVs [missiles] onto its missiles in silos) leaving the START-2 treaty, creating hypersonic missiles that allegedly can break through any American missile defense system, introducing new *Topol*-Ms mobile ICBMs that also allegedly can break those defenses, and testing the *Bulava* SLBM with similar characteristics. Still Moscow apparently thought this was not enough, and only 6 weeks after Lavrov's public complaints in Japan, Vice-Premier Sergei Ivanov called for nuclear parity with Washington, even though the quest for such parity would undoubtedly undermine Russia's economy unless he meant the retention of strategic stability, albeit at unequal numbers of missiles. Nevertheless, the real threat for Moscow here is the U.S. policy to build missile defenses and an alliance excluding Russia and China, not Japanese missile defenses. Those defenses are mainly directed formally against North Korean missiles and in reality the threat of Chinese missiles, not Russia.

Russian experts long ago noted that the military balance in East Asia was unfavorable to Russia and specifically invoked the specter of Russia losing its nuclear naval potential there.[251] That nuclear naval potential remains precarious as Moscow recently admitted that its submarines conducted a total of three patrols in 2007.[252] To overcome these weaknesses and threats, and thanks to Russia's economic resurgence (largely energy-driven, however), then President Vladimir Putin and Deputy Prime Minister and former Defense Minister Sergei Ivanov announced a planned strategic upgrade for the Pacific Fleet, specifically aiming to address this problem and make the Fleet Russia's primary naval strategic component.[253] This policy reverses prior naval policy that made Russia's Northern Fleet the strategic bastion for anti-American scenarios in the 1990s, testifying to an enhanced threat perception in Asia. The recent expansion of Russian military activity in and around the Arctic, including calls to incorporate Arctic scenarios into Russia's armed forces' training and doctrine, should be seen, at least in part, in this context despite the recent Russian show of force in the Arctic.[254] Here we should understand that Russia's forces, particularly those in the North and the Far East, may be deployed on a "swing basis" where either the Fleet, or air forces, or even nuclear forces in one theater move to support the analogous forces in the other. The Northern Fleet, a nuclear armed fleet, as a swing fleet can go to challenge enemies from the North Pacific, presumably from bastions in the Kola Peninsula. Similarly, the Pacific Fleet has its bastions from which it may be tasked to conduct missions in the Arctic.

Alternatively, the Northern Fleet and Russian Air forces based in the high north can be used to sweep the North Pacific of enemy air and naval assets. Russia has carried out exercises whereby one fleet moves to the aid of the other under such a concept.[255] Likewise, Russia has rehearsed scenarios for airlifting ground forces from the North to the Pacific in order to overcome the "tyranny of distance" that makes it very difficult for Russia to sustain forces in Northeast Asia. And the revival of regular air patrols over the oceans have clearly involved the Pacific-based units of the nuclear-capable Long Range Aviation forces as well as some of the air forces based in the North and Arctic who fly in the areas around Alaska.[256] Similarly, nuclear exercises moving forces or targeting weapons from the North to the Pacific or vice versa have also occurred.[257] To the degree that Arctic Missions become part of the regular repertoire of the Russian armed forces, they will also to some degree spill over into the North Pacific.

As part of this strategy, President Medvedev announced in September 2008 that Russia would not only build space defenses but that a guaranteed nuclear deterrent system for both military and political circumstances (which are not explained or defined) must be built by 2020. He also announced the construction of warships, mainly nuclear submarines armed with cruise missiles (which are unregulated by any convention or agreement and thus able to do whatever Moscow wants with them) and multipurpose submarines.[258] The Pacific Fleet will be the main fleet and one of two nuclear fleets (the Northern Fleet) will be the other, suggesting that the main mission of that fleet is to provide a reliable second-strike deterrent while the non-nuclear vessels will protect the "boomers" (nuclear armed submarines) and prevent hostile forces from coming within their range. Meanwhile, Russia's long-term rearmament program apparently envisions the renewal of the submarine fleet as nuclear propelled multirole submarines, in an effort to save money. Three missions for them will be anti-submarine warfare, anti-aircraft carrier missions (mainly against U.S. carrier battle groups), and attacking surface ships and transports. The submarines that are not equipped with SLBMs will be armed with precision conventional weapons to be a strategic non-nuclear deterrence force.[259] Nonetheless and even though the Far East is very much a naval theater, Moscow's main investments through 2010 will evidently go not so much to the Navy as to nuclear weapons (to redress Russia's conventional inferiority vis-à-vis U.S. and Chinese threats) and to air and air defense in order to forestall a Kosovo-like aerial campaign.[260] This emphasis on strengthening the nuclear deterrent, especially the sea-based deterrent, in the Asia-Pacific is clearly a response to both missile defenses and the augmentation of America's nuclear and conventional long-range strike forces in an effort to maintain deterrence and strategic stability in that theater.

This strategy also connects to Moscow's concerns about the conventional equation because it cannot stand up for a long time, especially in an austere economy of force theater that must be self-sustaining against large-scale conventional attacks over very exposed and huge borders. Consequently, at some point nuclear weapons, possibly TNW's or *Iskander's* or the *Skorost'* system, might have to be called into play to redress that balance and restore control over intrawar escalation. At the conventional level, apart from ongoing reinforcement or resupply of the forces with what is hoped to be more advanced conventional weapons and improved training and quality of the manpower (a very dubious assumption given the inability and refusal to build a truly professional army), reform also entails experiments in new force structures and rapid reaction forces. Moscow is endeavoring to develop a functioning mechanism of rapid response and airlift (the idea of the swing fleet or forces also plays here) from the North or interior of Russia to threatened sectors of the theater.

Second, Russia, as in Central Asia, is building an integrated, mobile, and all arms, if not combined arms, force consisting of land, air, and sea forces capable of dealing with failing state scenarios, insurgencies, terrorism, scenarios involving large-scale criminal activities, and ultimately conventional attack. Third, if, however, the scale of the threat overwhelms or is too large for the conventional forces, doctrine evidently continues to point to the use of nuclear weapons (probably TNW or *Iskander,* or other NSNW) in a first-strike or possibly even preventive mode, as stated by Baluyevsky.[261] On January 20, 2008, he stated that "We do not intend to attack anyone, but we consider it necessary for all our partners in the world community to clearly understand . . . that to defend the sovereignty and territorial integrity of Russia and its allies, military forces will be used, including preventively, including with the use of nuclear weapons."[262] Russian commentators noted that he was speaking entirely within the parameters of established Russian doctrine, and that he essentially conceded the failure of conventional forces to provide adequate defense and deterrence at the high end of the spectrum of conflict.[263] But beyond that, Baluyevsky invoked the use of nuclear weapons in a first or preventive strike to defend allies. By allies, he probably meant largely the CIS states to whom Moscow has extended its nuclear umbrella. But in the context of Russia's Asia-Pacific territories, his remarks bring us to the political dimensions of Russia's efforts to overcome the strategic challenges it faces there.

Those are not only U.S. challenges. Northeast Asia's nuclear landscape is changing under pressure of Korean proliferation and China's rise. This could present Russia with difficult choices, especially given its nuclear and conventional deficiencies. As the pressure on China to abandon its no first use policy grows along with its nuclear and apparent second-strike capability, Russian strategy must factor these new trends into account even as it must reduce its nuclear forces.[264] This downward pressure on the Far East's regional arsenal was already apparent in 2004-05, and, if Baluyevsky's remarks are to be taken seriously, it is likely that the Northern Fleet's nuclear forces and Russia's NSNW will become more important for consideration of deterrence or first strike in the Asian as well as European theater. As of 2004:

> Currently, about 20% of the deployed Russian strategic nuclear forces remain in the Eastern part of Russia. As strategic forces shrink, the pace of reductions in the region is the fastest. In particular, three of the four divisions of the Russian Strategic Forces that have been disbanded since 2000 were located here. And the reductions will continue. Most likely, the SS-18 base at Uzhur will be closed down after 2010. The future of the SS-25 mobile intercontinental ballistic missiles (ICBMs) is also uncertain, as they are getting older. The submarine base on the Kamchatka peninsula will likely no longer host strategic submarines once the last Delta-III nuclear submarines will be retired. Thus, perhaps, the only place where strategic forces will remain in this part of Russia is Ukrainka, the home of strategic bombers. As deployment of strategic nuclear forces in the Eastern part of Russia is curtailed, non-strategic nuclear weapons in the region may be assigned a stronger role. According to the author's assessment, nearly one third of the 3,300 Russian non-strategic weapons are assigned for deployment with general-purpose forces in the Siberian and Far Eastern military districts. All of these weapons are currently kept at central storage facilities of the 12th Directorate of the Russian Armed Forces. In case of hostilities they can be deployed with surface-to-surface, surface-to-air, air-to-surface, anti-ship, antisubmarine missiles, and other dual-use means of the Ground, Air, and Naval Forces.[265]

However, if nuclear missions grow in importance and likely consideration, this will inhibit North Korea's disposition to give up its existing nuclear weapons, not to mention foregoing new nuclear weapons. Similarly, Japan and South Korea will either be further tempted to go nuclear or cleave ever more to Washington, which would likely increase its regional military presence under such conditions.[266] Therefore, a purely military and preeminently nuclear strategy leads Russia into a strategic dead end here. A political strategy is essential and even paramount in Russia's endeavors to defuse potential security challenges here.

Such a strategy is even more essential because of the problems generated by China's overall military and nuclear buildup. First of all, there are multiplying signs that the no first use injunction in Chinese military doctrine is neither as absolute a ban as China has previously proclaimed and that it is under pressure from younger officers there.[267] Thus China is now debating retention of its no first use posture regarding nuclear weapons and nuclear weapons appear to be playing a more prominent role in Chinese strategy than was hitherto believed to be the case. For example, China is building a hitherto undisclosed nuclear submarine base in the Pacific and a major nuclear base in its interior, moves that suggest consideration of a second strike capability but can also put much pressure on Russia's Pacific Fleet and Russian Asia.[268]

Russian military analysts or planners are quite aware of the possibility of Chinese military threats even though they do not discuss them often unless they are critical of the partnership with China or profess to believe, as is apparently now the case, that they have at least 10 years before China can be a real threat and that China is not now a real threat to Russia.[269] Even so, at least some writers have pointed out that the rise in China's capabilities could go beyond a conventional threat to Russian assets in Siberia and Russian Asia. For example, the following 2004 analysis took into account both the limited nuclear capability China had then and the possibilities that could subsequently ensue based on those forces' ongoing development.

> Despite the significant qualitative makeup of the current Chinese nuclear missile potential, its combat capabilities are quite limited; it would hardly be adequate to destroy highly protected command and control posts and could not substantially degrade Russia's ground and sea-based strategic nuclear forces. However, this potential would be capable of substantially degrading the Russian Federation Armed Forces group in the Far Eastern Theater of Military Operations and of doing major damage to the population and economy not only in the Far Eastern and Urals regions, but even in the Central Region of European Russia. According to available data, so far China does not have missile systems with MIRVed warheads, but the upsurge in activity related to the building of antimissile defense systems could accelerate its development of that type of weapons system, including antimissile defense countermeasures. It should be noted that the PRC's economic and technological potential is quite adequate for a quantitative and qualitative breakthrough in the area of its strategic offensive weapons development.[270]

Given these aforementioned trends, we might well see a rethinking of Russia's nuclear strategy in Asia.[271]

These trends in China's military development fuel Moscow's aforementioned ambivalence about the INF treaty. As Russian officials from Putin down have argued, other countries to Russia's south and east are building such missiles but America and Russia are debarred from doing so. In October 2007,

> Mr. Putin said that Russia would leave the INF treaty unless it was turned into a global agreement to constrain other states, including those "located in our near vicinity." He did not identify any country but Iran and North Korea are within the range covered by the treaty. Dmitri Peskov, a Kremlin spokesman, later acknowledged that

China, India and Pakistan had medium-range missile capabilities. He insisted that Mr. Putin was concerned about an imbalance of regional security rather than any specific threat.[272]

But these remarks also reveal that Moscow cannot publicly reveal or confront its true threat perceptions and instead blames Washington for its failure to take Russian interests into account. Thus while Moscow had "privately told Washington it wanted medium range missiles to counter Iranian threats, it publicly argued that the lack of Iranian missiles meant the U.S. did not need a defense system."[273]

From here we can see that from Moscow's standpoint, American missile defenses not only threaten it directly, they also force it to "lean to one side," i.e., become partners of China, which is regarded as a lesser threat, more predictable, and more respectful of Russian interests. As Deputy Foreign Minister Aleksandr Losyukov said in 2007,

We would like to see a non-circuited system. Besides, we might make our own contribution to it, too. Then we would have no reason to suspect this system is targeted against us — If it is true that the system being created is expected to ward off some threats posed by irresponsible regimes, then it is not only Europe, the United States or Japan that one should have to keep in mind. When some other countries' concerns are kept outside such a system, they may have the feeling threats against them are growing, too. Consequently, the systems to be created must accommodate the concerns of other countries concerned.[274]

Clearly the other countries to which he refers are Russia and China, both of whom feel that America disregards their interests and concerns. Thus it is not surprising that Russia publicly criticized the U.S.-Japan collaboration on missile defenses and the linking of Australia to the U.S-Japanese alliance about which it had previously been silent. Here Moscow has adopted China's argument, for certainly the U.S. alliance system is not primarily targeted on Russia. Such arguing on behalf of mainly Chinese interests suggests that as part of the Sino-Russian partnership, we are beginning to encounter the phenomenon that many Russian analysts warned about, specifically that Russia ends up following China's line. But this may well be because Russia perceives that Washington will not grant it the self-inflated status that it claims for itself either in Europe or in Asia. Interestingly enough, while China, according to most analysts, had hitherto been seen as desisting from challenging the U.S. missile defense program by a vigorous program of building nuclear weapons, Russia seems ready to do so even though the utility of that program for its overall interests, which normally focus on getting the West to include it as a major international actor, is decidedly moot.[275]

Even if one argues or warns that Russia's strategic partnership with China resembles an alliance that could fracture Asia into bipolarity, this partnership may be based more on what both sides oppose than on a shared positive view of world politics.[276] Certainly it still lacks a solid economic underpinning. Therefore Beijing's growing quest for a global role may leave Russia behind. Certainly Beijing appears to be pressing Moscow for more tangible signs of support like increased energy shipments and support for its attacks on the U.S.-Japanese alliance. Although Moscow obliged somewhat in 2007, it is once again making overtures to Japan, having suddenly decided that

Japanese missile defense is not aimed against it and failing to send China the energy it needs and wants.[277]

Indeed, the alliance or comity with China presents great strategic problems for Russia because of the risk of dependence upon China that it inevitably carries. While Russia needs China as a partner in Asia against American power and policy, it also covertly depends upon America's alliance system to maintain a balance there, forestall a renationalization of Japanese defense policy, and give it an opportunity to remind Beijing that because of its independence it can undertake a rapprochement with Japan. Moscow has played off Beijing and Tokyo regarding the destination of energy pipelines to the Asia-Pacific, and in 1997 Defense Minister Igor Rodionov praised the U.S. alliance system in a not so subtle reminder by both Tokyo and Moscow to China that Russia had a Japanese option if it cared to exercise it. Such divide and rule tactics are basic to Russian foreign policy.[278] Since Moscow now proclaims that its foreign policy will consist of purely tactical alliances with interested parties, it may yet turn out that Russia outsmarts itself and will not be fully trusted by any major interlocutor in Asia. [279] Absent a vision of the regional order other than its returning as a great power, Russia might yet find itself isolated and distrusted.

Yet weighing all the alternatives in the balance, Russia has made up its mind to react.[280] It perceives U.S. nuclear policy and strategy as part of an overarching strategy to isolate and threaten it and is responding accordingly, asymmetrically as promised. Thus its response is partnership, if not alliance with China, pressure on Japan to desist from targeting Russia with its missile defenses coupled with alternating offers of economic incentives for partnership in the region, and the nuclearization of the Pacific Fleet to ensure robust deterrence and a second-strike capability.

The issue of missile defenses in Europe raises different problems for Russia. Despite all the ink and hysteria it has spilled and displayed on this issue, Moscow's claims that these systems are targeted against its nuclear weapons, threaten its basic interests, and that Washington is not being forthcoming about the details or negotiations are utterly mendacious. Even anti-American military writers and analysts acknowledge this. For instance, writing in 2001, we find a group of leading military men and civilian analysts headed by retired General Makhmut A. Gareyev, the doyen of Russian military thinking and President of the Academy of Military Sciences, writing together that,

> We are conscious of the fact that even if the U.S.A. starts creating an antimissile defense system, it will hardly present a threat to our nuclear potential for years and years to come. The point rather is this: a collapse of the ABM Treaty is likely to strike a blow to all disarmament agreements as it may to the non-proliferation and strategic stability regimes in general. And this is what may represent a serious challenge to the security of both Russia and, incidentally the U.S.A. (something we are telling the U.S. side).[281] (Italics in the original)

From the Russian point of view stated earlier in this monograph, it is the threat to strategic stability as Moscow understands it that is the real threat which Washington should take seriously. But it has been lost in a flurry of mendacious charges about phantom military threats and charges. Russia got 10 detailed technical briefings on the subject before 2007 so it is hardly uninformed as to the capacities of these systems. Ten radars and interceptors in Poland and the Czech

Republic cannot threaten Moscow's nuclear forces in any way or fashion, especially as their trajectories do not intersect with those of Russian missiles. Neither are the repeated claims from Putin on down that Iran is not building an atom bomb or that it has no IRBM capability and will not have one for years truthful as Moscow itself knows.[282]

In fact both Deputy Prime Minister and former Defense Minister Sergei Ivanov and former Chief of Staff General Yuri N. Baluyevsky have acknowledged Iran's threats.[283] Commenting on Iran's launch in early 2007 of a suborbital weather rocket, Lieutenant General Leonid Sazhin stated that "Iran's launch of a weather rocket shows that Tehran has not given up efforts to achieve two goals—create its own carrier rocket to take spacecraft to orbit and real medium-range combat missiles capable of hitting targets 3,000-5,000 miles away."[284]

Although he argued that this capability would not fully materialize for 3-5 years, it would also take at least that long to test and deploy the American missile defenses that are at issue. Equally significantly, Major-General Vitaly Dubrovin, a Russian space defense expert, said flatly "now Tehran has a medium-range ballistic missile capable of carrying a warhead."[285] Naturally both men decried the fact that Iran appears intent on validating American threat assessments.[286] Since they wrote in February 2007, Iran has announced that it has developed the *Ashura* IRBM with a 2,000Km range.[287] Indeed Putin's 2007 proposal for joint use of the Gabala air and missile defense installation in Azerbaijan implicitly acknowledged the validity of the U.S. threat perception concerning Iran. As one Iranian newspaper wrote in September 2007,

Meanwhile, the change of stance by Russia regarding the anti-missile defense shield, from criticizing it and rejecting it to proposing the use of an alternative site for that system, could be regarded as a remarkable development that indicates the serious threats posed by that project. In the case of the implementation of a "joint missile defense system" and the installation of intercepting radar systems in our neighboring countries—the Republic of Azerbaijan, Turkey, Iraq, or Kuwait—would include the intensification of American threats against our country.[288]

To understand Moscow's alarm and anxiety about these missile defenses, we must look at the scenarios advanced by Russian spokesmen as to why these defenses allegedly threaten Russia.

- As Dmitri Trenin has suggested, Moscow believes (though with no basis in fact—author) that the building of missile defenses represents an American perception of threats from Russian nuclear missiles. Therefore, these defenses aim to neutralize them in potential conflict.[289] Either Russian missiles would be attacked by a conventional air and space first strike, possibly involving these networks in Europe, or else these missile defenses would frustrate a retaliatory second strike, leaving Russia defenseless.[290]
- While these missile defenses in and of themselves are no threat, they represent the first stage of a planned or potential U.S. buildup of a missile network in Europe that could then neutralize Russia's first and/or second strike capabilities as cited above and shift the burden of war to Russia and Europe.[291]
- If missile defenses were stationed at these bases, that would be a pretext for then stationing offensive missiles there, which would force

Moscow to assume the worst case scenario. In turn, that could cause Russia to attempt to shoot them down, leading to a conflict with America.[292]

- As suggested above, these defenses and whatever may follow them rupture the fabric of strategic stability where neither side has the freedom of action or margin of superiority that might encourage it to think it could employ coercive diplomacy or military force with impunity. That strategic stability equation is of critical importance to Russia because it believes that otherwise Washington might be tempted to think it has a margin within which it could strike at Russia with relative impunity.

- Finally there is a fifth, and always unstated but critical aspect here. These defenses entrench the United States in Europe's military defense and foreclose any prospect of Moscow's being able to intimidate or reestablish its hegemony over Eastern and Central Europe, and even possibly the CIS. If missile defenses exist in Europe, threats like TNW and the *Iskander* are greatly diminished, if not negated. Because empire and the creation of a fearsome domestic enemy are the justifications for and inextricable corollary of autocracy at home, the end of empire impels the decline of Russia as a great power, or so it is imagined, and generates tremendous pressure for domestic reform. As Lilia Shevtsova writes,

Maintaining Russia's superpower ambitions and the domination of the former Soviet space are now crucial to the reproduction of the political system and the self-perpetuation of power. In short, Russia's foreign policy has become an important tool for achieving the Kremlin's domestic objectives. And a key foreign policy objective is to create the image of a hostile international environment and demonstrate a strong reaction to which it can legitimize the hyper-centralization of Kremlin power, top-down governance, and its crackdown on political pluralism.[293]

Missile defenses contribute greatly to shattering the tie between autocracy and empire, and, if Moscow cannot dominate the CIS as it hopes to do, its domestic form of government no longer has any legitimate or even pseudo-legitimate justification since its avowed purpose is to restore Russia as a great power. Moreover, autocracy cannot survive in a democratic Europe. Arguably, this is the real threat, not the highly unlikely threat of a war in Europe.

Therefore we see Russia's constant and habitual resort to intimidation of any and all states who may be tempted to join NATO or host these systems. Those tactics of intimidation are clearly Mafia-like tactics, and evoke the classic signs of a protection racket. It is not for nothing that many European diplomats and intelligence officials characterize Russia in just this way, i.e., as a Mafia state.[294] In other words, it appears to be a key belief of the Russian elite that because of its presupposition of conflict with the West, it must retain a formidable capability for holding Europe hostage militarily as well as through energy and conventional military power. ICBMs and SLBMs can do this but they also have to deter Washington. Where threats to Europe are concerned TNW, including systems like the *Iskander* and *Skorost'* ballistic missiles and possibly the cruise missile version of the *Iskander* (*Iskander-K*), are intended for that purpose as well as for purposes of a nuclear first strike with which to restore control over the intrawar escalation process. Even a rudimentary American military presence in Europe is anathema to Russian plans as it entrenches the U.S. overall military presence and extended deterrence in Europe and creates stronger European solidarity. Since two clear themes in Russian discourse about Europe are, first, that the American presence is unnatural and that by placing missile defense there, Washington is embroiling Europe in unnecessary and unwanted conflicts; and, second, that European solidarity is "silly" and a complicating factor for Russia, missile defense undermines many of Russia's political objectives for European security as well as their cognitive basis.[295] And no government welcomes such developments.

Russian Replies to Missile Defenses.

True to the spirit of a policy based on deterrence and the presupposition of mutual hostility with Washington, Russia is either unable or unwilling to follow Washington's move from deterrence vis-à-vis Russia towards a defense-dominant world with lower numbers of nuclear weapons, especially offensive ones. Instead, Russia is building up or attempting to build up more capable and newer offensive missiles with professed capabilities to evade any and all manner of defenses. Medvedev's recent demands for a comprehensive deterrent against all contingencies by 2020 when missile defenses are supposed to be fully in place only reaffirm that hostile posture.[296] Such action-reaction processes betray the fact that Russia and its generals have regressed back to a period before Gorbachev's reforms in their thinking and cannot or will not seem to understand, as do civilian analysts, that remaining in this posture and demanding strategic stability and some notion of parity with America is not only a bankrupt economic policy, but also a bankrupt strategy that only replicates mutual hostility.[297] Indeed, Baluyevsky admitted in 2005 that, "The nuclear potential of the armed forces of the Russian Federation is currently formed up to the agreed level of minimum sufficiency."[298] These remarks show how hard, even ruinous, a task it is for Russia to sustain multiple missile programs.

According to Russian sources, in the last 7 years Moscow has undertaken the following moves in response to the U.S. withdrawal from the ABM treaty and move to construct defenses on its Pacific coast and now in Europe. In 2007 Ivanov unveiled plans to build by that date: 50 new *Topol-M* ICBM missile complexes on mobile launchers; 34 new silo-based *Topol-M* missiles and control units; 50 new bombers; and 31 ships and to fully rearm 40 tank, 97 infantry, and 50 parachute battalions. Forty *Topol-M* silo-based missiles have already been deployed. In 2007 alone, the military would get 17 new ballistic missiles, rather than four a year as has recently been the case, and four spacecraft and booster rockets. It would overhaul a long-range aviation squadron, six helicopter and combat aviation squadrons, seven tank and 13 motor rifle battalions. In 2007 alone, $11 billion will be spent on new weapons. Thirty-one new ships will be commissioned, including eight SSBN's carrying ICBMs (presumably the forthcoming *Bulava* missile). And in 2009-10, Russia will decide whether or not to build a new shipyard for the construction of aircraft carriers. Over this period, 50 Tu-160 *Blackjack* and Tu-95 *Bear* strategic bombers would operate as well. Doctrinally, Russia will also retain its right of launching preemptive strikes.[299] The increase of the original military budget for 2009 by

27 percent, the extensive nuclear building plans and demands for more nuclear submarines (both in terms of engine propulsion and weapons) suggest a reversion to the kind of thinking that preceded Gorbachev.[300]

In this connection, it is clear and admitted by Solovtsov that in 2002, once America exited the ABM treaty, Russia altered the development plan for its strategic nuclear forces to emphasize the creation of fundamentally new and effective means of penetrating any missile system. Apart from the *Topol-M* (SS-27) mobile ICBM, which will be, if it has not already been, MIRVed, there is the new land-based ICBM, the RS-24, that was tested in 2007. This ICBM is fitted with a multiple reentry vehicle so it is capable of being MIRVed up to apparently 10 missiles and will replace the aging SS-19 and SS-20. The *Iskander* family of missiles has already been discussed above, but it, too, is part of this process, especially the cruise missile version. Medvedev's recent call for these nuclear submarines to be armed with (presumably) nuclear cruise missiles suggests as well a demand for or the expected existence of a submarine launched version of the *Iskander-K* discussed above. Moscow is also maintaining existing missile complexes as long as it can through the parameters of the State Armaments Program through 2015.[301] And since Medvedev is now calling for building through 2020 for the navy and the nuclear forces, we can expect that this program will continue through that date as well. The naval nuclear forces have built two new missiles, the *Sineva* and the *Bulava*, and has launched new submarine programs e.g., the *Delta IV* class SSBN from which the *Sineva* was tested (specifically the *Tula*) in 2007 and the *Borey*-Class submarine, e.g., the *Yuri Dolgoruki*, for the *Bulava*. But despite introduction of these weapons, the *Bulava* has failed its recent tests and has not yet been introduced. Meanwhile the *Topol-M* will only be introduced at the rate of six or seven a year, which evidently is the limit of Russian capabilities.[302] Even so, all of these new weapons have as their aim the evasion or penetration of U.S. missile defenses.[303]

But Russian ambitions do not end here. Russian writers previously talked about hypersonic missiles. It is not clear if any of the new ones listed here include such capabilities. But there is no doubt that the intention to build such missiles is probably still there, and that work on them is moving forward. Second, Russia has announced tests of a precision guided 2,000Km cruise missile and is having its strategic bombers test cruise missile launches. Finally, Russia is also developing a low-trajectory ICBM (this may refer to the RS-24 which is supposed to be able to penetrate enemy missile defenses).[304] Such programs underscore the fact that inasmuch as the U.S. missile defenses in Europe will not be up until 2011 or 2013, there is no threat to Russian missiles.

Nevertheless, as noted above, at present Moscow cannot defend against an air-space attack, some parts of its country not yet being capable of affording coverage by air defenses, and Putin has opposed investment in missile defenses saying in 2004 that it is premature to invest large sums in that program.[305] Likewise, there is mounting doubt about the credibility of Russia's naval nuclear forces.[306] While this doubt seems misplaced, at least for the next decade, if the *Borey*-class submarines and accompanying missiles are built, it is noteworthy that Stephen Cimbala's analysis of this issue also suggests movement towards cruise missiles and cites Russian reports of a new missile that surpasses the *Topol-M* and that should be operational by 2017.

Perhaps this missile could be used for both land-based and sea-based deterrents.[307] Medvedev's call for a new nuclear naval program may reflect that disquiet among Russian elites about this leg of the triad.[308]

Meanwhile, at present, in fact, Russia actually has no adequate response to American missile defenses as former commander of the radio-technical troops of Russian Air Defense Lieutenant General Grigory Dubrov has admitted.[309] Worse yet, major military figures, e.g., Gareyev, are pressing for the forthcoming defense doctrine to emphasize that Russia developed its defense posture on the assumption that the "nuclear weapons of practically all major states are ultimately intended against Russia."[310] Even worse news for Russia is the reduction of the nuclear component under Putin. Boris Yeltsin bequeathed to Putin land, sea, and air based warheads totaling 5,842. As of 2007, according to the National Strategy Institute, Russia has 3,344 warheads. Thus it has lost 405 platforms and 2,498 warheads. The situation in conventional weapons is no better. Under conditions where Russia's defense industry cannot make up this gap and can only produce 6-7 ICBMs a year, the gap between U.S. and Russian forces both quantitatively and qualitatively will inevitably widen.[311] And these considerations do not take into account the rise in Chinese conventional and nuclear power that Russia must also find a way to deter.

START AND RUSSIA'S STRATEGIC CHALLENGES

In this strategic environment and especially given the Russian official position of adhering to deterrence as a strategy and to the principle of strategic stability with Washington as a way of restraining it, Russia is facing ever more difficult strategic dilemmas despite its newfound wealth and status. Even if we left aside the Chinese factor, U.S. policy presents Russia with enormous, if not insuperable, challenges because America simply refuses to stay deterred and, as noted above, Russia evidently finds it increasingly difficult to deter the United States across both the conventional and nuclear spectrum. The dominant motif of U.S. defense policy, to some extent under President Clinton, but strongly articulated in the Bush administration is the refusal of the United States to accept any kind of deterrence upon its capabilities for global strike. This trend is unlikely to abate under the next administration. Apart from America's unchallenged capability for conventional power projection and global strike using long-range missiles and integrated land, sea, air, space, and cyber capabilities, it has undertaken the following initiatives with respect to nuclear weapons, all of which are seen from Moscow as either lowering the threshold for actual nuclear use on the battlefield or freeing itself from the constraints of arms control treaties, mutual transparency, and strategic stability.

- America has abandoned the ABM treaty and is building strategic defenses in lands Russia considers to be its sphere of influence. Given the opaque nature of U.S. missile defense development—consisting of an open-end system architecture and periodic block deployments—this process engenders strategic uncertainty rather than stabilizing transparency. This alarms Moscow into believing that these programs will not end with what is currently planned for construction in Poland and the Czech Republic. Thus as Dmitri Trenin writes,

Moscow's core problem with the U.S.BMD [ballistic missile defense] position area in Central Europe is that Russia regards it as part of the global network in an environment where it is not fully clear as to what Washington's long-term politico-military strategy toward Russia will be. The United States' de facto refusal to join Russia in building a joint Theater Missile Defense (TMD) system to protect Europe has been seen as a worrying sign; alleged U.S. backtracking on confidence-building measures for the Polish and Czech sites is another. The story planted in the Russian media in July 2008 about Moscow considering the use of Cuba by its strategic bombers, now again on global patrolling missions, is obviously sending a message to Washington that Russia sees the missile defense deployments, which it cannot reliably monitor, as a strategic challenge.[312]

- American military doctrine expressly calls for the use of nuclear weapons (which kind are not specified) in its global strike strategy even in a preemptive mode, and at the same time assigns potential missions of destroying an adversary's nuclear or C3I capability to advanced conventional weapons.[313] These doctrinal or mission assignments not only openly call for use of nuclear weapons in a first-strike mode on the battlefield, or as preemptive and preventive strike weapons, the use of conventional missiles atop nuclear missile launchers to accomplish nuclear missions could easily lead adversaries into assuming an incoming nuclear strike, especially if they, like Moscow, operate upon a launch on warning (LOW) basis.

- Despite all the rhetoric to the contrary and the talk of Russia being a partner *and enemy* and not the target of American nuclear weapons, in fact, close examination of the size and structure of that arsenal suggests that an attack on Russian missiles, i.e., a countervalue attack, is the canonical mission for which those forces are structured, a fact that makes the preceding points all the more dangerous.
- Whereas Russia is destroying or cannot replace nuclear weapons equal to the enhancement of U.S. conventional and nuclear capabilities, America, by walking out of the ABM treaty and refusing any kind of verification or constraint upon its ability to upload or replenish weapons, has a huge strategic nuclear reserve that can be quickly mobilized for military purposes.
- Despite the Bush administration's professions of faith that its Nuclear Posture Review (NPR) pointed to a movement away from reliance upon nuclear weapons, its presenter, Assistant Secretary of defense J. D. Crouch stated in 2002 that the United States would retain its triad, albeit at smaller quantitative levels, retain an "operationally deployed force" that could be augmented if the security environment changed, retain dismantled warheads so that the process of reductions could be reversed at any time if necessary, and still retain a capacity to "hold at risk a wide range of target types." Indeed, Crouch observed that while we regarded Russia as a nonthreatening power,

> Russia's nuclear forces and programs, nevertheless, remain a concern. Russia faces

many strategic problems around its periphery and its future course cannot be charted with certainty. U.S. planning must take this into account. In the event that U.S. relations with Russia significantly worsen in the future, the U.S. may need to revise its nuclear force levels and postures.[314]

We should take into account the fact that the unreformed defense establishment and the political leadership share an ingrained neo-Soviet reflex that the United States is and was the main enemy seeking to threaten Russia. Thus, as a forthcoming paper by Mikhail Tsypkin of the Naval Postgraduate School says,

The Russians have probably interpreted all of this as implicitly directed against Russia as well as likely other targets. The fact that the NPR was only partially declassified must have unshackled the imagination of GRU analysts, who could add their own projections to the information made available by the U.S. They also would not have missed the reference to future "defensive systems with multiple layers" in the leaked excerpts of the NPR.[315] The emphasis on precision strikes combined with enhanced intelligence against mobile targets must have left the Russians wondering about the survivability of Russia's mobile SS-25 and SS-27 (*Topol-M*) ICBMs, while the requirement to increase hard target-kill capability would make them think about the survivability of their country's silo-based ICBMs and command and control facilities.[316]

- Tsypkin also observes that reliable channels of communication, e.g., the Consultative Group for Strategic Stability (the original group of 2+2 of foreign and defense ministers and the working groups under it) were moribund from the moment of their creation in 2002. Moreover, U.S. plans were briefed to Moscow by assistant secretaries, a rank that in Russia does not connote high status or influence. This protocol gaffe may have added to Russians' sense that Putin was being deliberately snubbed. As a result, while there were American briefings on missile defense, there were apparently no senior-level *consultations* until the middle of 2007, another sign to Moscow of a deliberate disregard for its status and interests.[317]

- As a result of all the foregoing points, it would appear to Russia that America is moving towards a first-strike capability against Russia's nuclear missile sites integrating conventional, nuclear and, as suggested below space capabilities.

- Washington is also experimenting with or trying to build low-yield nuclear weapons that are so-called bunker busters that can again lower the threshold of nuclear use according to Russia and which can threaten deeply buried missile sites and C3I centers, e.g., Yammantau Mountain.

- Finally, Washington is also discussing, if not implementing, the emplacement of weapons in space, not just satellites or weapons that traverse rather than are based in space.[318] As we have seen, all of these moves, whether singly or as part of an integrated defense strategy, combine to provoke Russia into charging that the United States is threatening other states with nuclear weapons, undermining strategic stability, destroying deterrence and transparency, stimulating proliferation among threatened states, and forcing Russia (and for that matter China too) to develop their own nuclear and asymmetric capabilities to either hold Europe or Japan, Taiwan, and South Korea hostage and to cling ever more to a strategy of deterrence whose fundamental premise is the irreducible mutual hostility of the adversaries. Furthermore, albeit in different language and style, these Russian critiques are substantively very much the same as those mounted by such domestic critics of the Bush administration as Jonathan Schell, Hans Kristensen, David McDonough, Ivan Oelrich, Christopher Chyba, George Bunn, and others.[319] And these critics all base themselves on a close reading of the administration's own statements and official documents. If one looks at the results of the administration's strategy, the rise in proliferation, China's 25 percent increase in nuclear weapons since 2006, Russia's continuing adherence to a nuclear answer to its strategic problems vis-à-vis America, mounting hostility towards it, and the general decline of U.S. standing and power in the world, it should become clear that these criticisms have much merit.[320]

Similarly, under the circumstances, it should be clear why Russia wants to multilateralize not only the INF treaty but also a START treaty, and has been calling for that for the last 8 years.[321] Failing to understand this and failure to restore transparency and mutual confidence can only lead to an escalation of tensions and mutual suspicion, a reinforcement of the antidemocratic and neo-imperial trends in Russian foreign policy because the need to hold Europe hostage to Russian military and especially nuclear capability will grow as does the gap between Washington and Moscow. Worse yet, this failure will also enhance the likelihood of further nuclear proliferation as the two nuclear rivals and China compete across the globe for support.

As Cimbala has written, "The reassurance of a stable nuclear deterrence relationship between the U.S. and Russia, and at lower levels than hitherto, is a necessary condition for a viable nonproliferation regime and for crisis stability in a multipolar nuclear world."[322] A stable and secure bilateral relationship between these two states, founded on the kind of relationship deriving from nuclear reductions, is a necessary anchor for an international order in which proliferation is curtailed.[323] Absent such reassurance and such an anchor, we will all be sailing on very stormy seas without a rudder and with a corpse in the cargo.

RECOMMENDATIONS FOR THE OBAMA ADMINISTRATION

It will be noted here that the author is not recommending any particular force size or mixture for either Washington or Moscow. Instead, we and Russia need to consider fundamental strategic issues if we are to get back on track in curbing both the tendency to think of nuclear weapons as oversized and more effective conventional weapons and to restore the bilateral confidence and reassurance necessary for stabilizing unquiet regions and curbing proliferation. First, it is clear that the Bush administration's strategic unilateralism and willingness to entertain the use of nuclear weapons as warfighting weapons for theater scenarios against potential proliferators and in roles hitherto reserved for conventional ordnance has failed to achieve either security or U.S. interests. Predictably, it has instead achieved the reverse outcome: more nuclear weapons; a flight towards cruise missiles throughout Eurasia, including nuclear capable missiles like the *Iskander*; and a hardening of relations on these issues with Russia and China. Second, the rhetoric of partnership with Russia is not and has not been matched by changes in force structures even when such a partnership seemed feasible as in late 2001-03. As a result, the institutionalized logic of having nuclear missiles on both sides deployed against each other prevailed over arms control and those forces in both governments who cannot get out of the Cold War, particularly Moscow, where the elite is entrenched in its anti-Americanism and institutionally disposed to a paranoid view of enemies everywhere by virtue of its previous socialization in the Soviet KGB were able to prevail. The connection between the steady drift of the Putin regime towards domestic autocracy and its ingrained hostility to the West based on the aforementioned presupposition of conflict is quite strong.

Therefore, President Obama must approach issues of nuclear force structure, arms control, and Russia in a strategic manner in order to advance U.S. interests more efficaciously than has been the case during the Bush administration. Based on what both campaigns have said, they seem to want a new START treaty with major reductions and are willing to return to a robust but as yet unspecified verification regime. And they also support globalization of the INF treaty. To help them realize these goals, President Obama must undertake the following steps. First, he must quickly commission not just a negotiating team for these treaties whose time is running out, but also a full-fledged nuclear policy review. However, that review cannot be left solely to the Pentagon but must be controlled by him, or at least his direct agent, and involve other players, including civilian experts, so that the institutional pressure for maintaining an excessively large number of weapons and missions for them is countered by arguments that force credible answers in reply. This review must proceed concurrently with the START and INF treaty negotiations because of the deadlines attached to both treaties, which could expire in 2009.

This review or reviews should address the following questions: low-yield nuclear weapons as bunker buster weapons; the use of nuclear weapons in a first-strike, preventive, or even preemptive capability; the use of conventional missiles atop nuclear launchers to carry out missions hitherto of a nuclear nature; the development and deployment of the so called Reliable Replacement Weapon (RRW); the weaponization of space (that is, the placement of strike weapons as opposed to reconnaissance and C3I complexes in space that has long since happened), and the Comprehensive Test Ban Treaty (CTBT). In other words, the nature of our nuclear strategy and future force structure should be comprehensively rethought, with a view to taking into account broader strategic benefits and costs from adopting any or all of those policies pursued by the Bush administration. We make no a priori recommendations as to what the outcome or the recommendations of these reviews should be. But we do need to address whether or not we gain from pursuing these policies when the current strategic environment in all its dimensions and the interests of other major interlocutors are taken into account. The thoroughgoing unilateralism and ideological zeal of the Bush administration has led us, in regard to those issues, into a blind alley and united potential enemies against us, while diminishing our effective ability to advance our interests. These reviews should be conducted with cold analysis, not theological adherence to the belief that treaties either are a panacea or useless, that missile defense is a matter of theology either for good or bad, that unilateralism is always bad or alternatively always desirable, etc. The only criterion should be a coldly impartial look as to what degree adoption of any or all of these programs serve U.S. interests and to what degree and at what cost. We already see that these policies have intensified Russian (and Chinese) suspicions about our goals and objectives, leading them to greater collusion and obstruction of our overall foreign and defense policies. Surely, we can find an alternative to that self-defeating course of action and help move the debate from the frozen posture of deterrence with its inherent postulate of mutual hostility to a different defense-dominant and more inherently stabilizing discourse and policy.

Second, the Obama administration should support, as the presidential campaigns have, a reduction of strategic nuclear weapons — land, air, and sea-based — from the limits of the SORT treaty of 1,700-2,200 by 2012 to figures in the neighborhood of 1,000-1,200. We make no recommendations as to the size of each particular leg of the triad. Modeling of forces on both sides shows that they could ride out a first-strike at those numbers and still have sufficient retaliatory capability for a second-strike.[324] Third, as part of that treaty the new administration should support the restoration of the START I verification regime and also a ban on MIRVs, which the United States has long argued are destabilizing weapons. Certainly in the context of a new treaty and reductions, these weapons would be destabilizing. Fourth, the United States should support the Russian idea of multilateralizing these talks and the INF negotiations as well.

The reasons for supporting the multilateralization of these negotiations are quite obvious. It is long since time that China is acknowledged as a major nuclear power, with the attendant responsibilities thereof, i.e., fully participating in global arms control regimes. Hitherto China has been exempt from all these talks and treaties and has therefore been able to act without any external constraints in developing its nuclear forces. It also has thus been a free rider on the regimes crafted by these accords.[325] Consequently, it is necessary to persuade China to accept its new status and the responsibilities that go with its power and, equally importantly, to subject its nuclear program to legitimate international regulation. Persuading China to join both the INF and START processes would reduce the threat of nuclear and other wars around Taiwan and more generally throughout the Asia-Pacific region. The regulation and possible capping of China's nuclear forces would also reduce the pressure for missile defenses and the endless modernization of U.S. strategic forces in regions where Russia is particularly vulnerable. At the same time, recent articles claiming that the dispatch of the *Borey*-Class SSBN submarine with the *Bulava* missile to the Pacific Fleet where Russia is particularly vulnerable represents a riposte to missile defenses in Europe, showing the interactive dynamic at work in the question of missile defenses in both Europe and Asia.[326]

While it is doubtful that China will soon accede to these talks because they weaken or could even remove its trump card vis-à-vis the United States in a Taiwan or other scenario, China, not the United States, should bear the burden of refusing to move forward on nuclear disarmament. If China spurns these invitations, it also reveals that it wants a capability to hold both Russia and America hostage, a fact whose implications will not be lost on Russian policymakers and may slow the tendency to bandwagon with China, another development that would be entirely in the U.S. interest. On the other hand, were China to accede to participation in these two treaty regimes, we would finally be able to develop an independent and objective method for verifying Chinese nuclear deployments and developments, increase mutual confidence in Asia among at least the three major nuclear powers there, (America, Russia, and China), and reduce military threats throughout Asia and the Pacific. A third benefit of Chinese participation in these regimes would be the follow-on momentum that this would have vis-à-vis India and Pakistan. That momentum could slow the momentum of their arms race in regard to nuclear weapons, since Indian developments (which Pakistan follows) are to a considerable degree pegged to Chinese moves.[327]

There would be added benefits to globalizing the INF treaty, or at least supporting it. This globalization puts enormous pressure on Iran to stop its quest for nuclear weapons, for it would then lead to great pressure upon Iran to curtail its IRBM programs for the *Shahab-3*, a missile of 1,300Km range, the *Ashura*, a 2,000Km range, and the projected *Shahab-4* and *Shahab-5*, with ranges approaching intercontinental scope. If the INF process breaks down or cannot be globalized, then the way is open to revitalizing Putin's 2007 proposal for joint operation of missile defenses in Gabala and for a joint Russian-NATO Theater Missile Defense (TMD). Rather than have Russia walk out of the INF, which is its legal right, and thereby provoke a massive arms race in Europe and Asia, we should use this opportunity to move to a defense-dominant relationship in Eurasia consonant with broader strategic objectives sketched out below. Under those circumstances, the missile defenses currently being built in Poland and the Czech Republic would cease to be a problem for Russia. Instead they become a defense against Iran and the range of threats Iran could conceivably mount against Russia. This would be a much cheaper and more strategically effective way for Russia to deal with IRBM threats from Iran, and it would also have a restraining impact upon Chinese developments.

The prospect of meaningful strategic cooperation with Russia also weakens those in the Kremlin who base all policies on the initial premise of unending American hostility and readiness for war so that they can demand ever more resources from the Russian people for their own personal and institutional benefit. At the same time, such accords strengthen those who want to see more great power cooperation. Furthermore, moves that reorient the bilateral relationship from one of mutual deterrence that postulates an ingrained hostility with force structures to match that presumption towards a defense-dominant regime also weaken the intellectual and cognitive base of those who believe in inherent conflict, while strengthening forces wanting to work for more genuine partnership. At the same time, if a new INF treaty is achieved, the Russians will then have to choose between it and the United States on the one hand, and support for Iran on the other. New arms control treaties have proven in general to exercise great pressure globally to desist from proliferation, so a new INF treaty would likely not be an exception to this rule. A renewed INF treaty should then place Iran under considerable pressure to renounce its IRBMs, and without those programs, its quest for nuclear weapons becomes quite senseless.

At the same time, a new START treaty would also have similar effects globally, especially if China is part of it. A new START treaty would also certainly strengthen the prospects for a successful round of the next Preparatory Committee meetings of the Nonproliferation Treaty in 2010 as well as pressure on would-be proliferators. It would show both Beijing and Moscow that we take their concerns and status seriously, and that we can restore a significant measure of mutual confidence in our relations through a process of negotiations and of adherence to strict verification regimes. As part of that START process, we should also encourage the big five nuclear powers and members of the UN Security Council (UNSC) to move away from the hostility-inducing posture of mutual deterrence to a defense–dominant paradigm buttressed by treaties, inspection regimes, and robust but reduced second-strike capabilities that would be sufficient for retaliatory purposes and missions. As the United States is the strongest, most capable, and most advanced conventional military power in the world, it is entirely to its interests that it find a way to reduce as far as possible the possibility that nuclear weapons will be used as warfighting weapons, as they negate our comparative advantage. All these moves in regard to strategic weapons would also take away ammunition from Russia's hawks who still hanker after a Soviet-type military and nuclear force, complete with a Soviet threat assessment that does not answer the real threats to Russian security and bankrupts the country while lining the pockets of its despots and their retainers.

If we can regenerate this virtuous circle of successfully concluded INF and START treaties, we can then address the issue of the missile defenses in the Czech Republic and Poland. Our analysis has shown that irrespective of the Bush administration's strategies, which induced much anxiety in Moscow, Russia, as part of its strategy, insists on being able to intimidate Europe through the *Iskander*, especially its cruise missile variant and its TNW or NSNW. The threats of missile strikes and targeting that Moscow has made against virtually every state from the Baltic states to Georgia demonstrate the need for both missile defenses and, frankly, for NATO's continuing robustness, if not enlargement to states who want to join it on its terms, e.g., Ukraine and Georgia. As part of the next admininstration's arms control and Russian strategy, it should be made crystal clear to Russia that, as a matter of principle, it cannot claim partnership with Europe while threatening it and trying to intimidate it. Furthermore, that if it persists in doing so, we and our allies will take the necessary steps, even within a defense-dominant nuclear framework, to deter and rebuff those threats so that Russia pays the price of its misconceived and aggressive policies.

Accordingly, in regard to the nuclear agenda, the next administration, as part of its aforementioned moves towards a new INF and START treaty, should also make every effort to devise a workable verification regime for TNW or NSNW (this regime would also include the definitional issues that are crucial here in defining just what kind of weapons are being discussed) with a view towards eliminating not only these weapons on both sides, but also banning the use of cruise missiles like the *Iskander*-K in Europe. In other words, the administration should move beyond Russia's proposal, which may not be wholly serious (i.e., regarding the INF), to demand a Europe freed from the weapons covered by the INF. A mutually devised verification regime, along with defenses like the proposed joint U.S.-Russian defenses, would then ensure stability for both sides and eliminate any nuclear or missile threats against European governments. However, for this to work, Russia has to come back to the CFE treaty. So the U.S. Government in 2009 should hold to the CFE treaty and induce a Russian signature of the treaty contingent upon Russian withdrawals from Georgia and Moldova, which could then be the trigger for a general European ratification of that treaty that would restore its strict and confidence-building verification regime.

If consummated, these arms control measures would ratify the debellicization of Europe, which is the outstanding achievement of the last generation. If Russia refuses to go along with them, it will simply demonstrate conclusively that its quest for "sovereign democracy" is nothing more than a quest for empire in Eurasia, whose corollary is the intimidation of Europe and the bifurcation of Eurasia into blocs that are intrinsically hostile to each other. While this renewed regional bipolarity is not in Russia's or our interest, it is a threat that is well within our, NATO's, and the EU's capability to deter and even defeat. Here again, the idea is to take serious account of Russia's security concerns, but to use them to advance American and Western interests, while also inducing Russia to move from a hostile-based deterrence paradigm to a defense-dominant one that is not based on the presupposition of conflict. Then it would be clear that if there are threats to European security, they emanate from Moscow, not Washington. Essentially Russia will be given a choice of alternatives so that its demands for partnership and security, along with a "system-forming role," are taken account of but, from the U.S. view, harnessed to broader aims of peace, stability, and even progress towards democratization in both Europe and Asia.

Finally, our efforts to forge with Russia a viable, enduring, and mutually beneficial arms control regime as part of a new international order must be part of a broader comprehensive strategy toward Russia that addresses regional security, democracy, and energy, as well as arms control. All these policies must move together towards persuading Russia by force of circumstances (not circumstances of force) to rethink its fundamental postulates concerning both its domestic political order and the international political order within which it takes part. In engaging Russian proposals for arms control seriously, we must demand an equivalent serious engagement with our agenda that comprises the issues listed above. I have elsewhere described what that agenda should look like and what its prerequisites for success are, so there is no need to repeat all of them again here.[328]

However, it must be stressed that while U.S. policy will change out of necessity in 2009, though we cannot forecast at present the direction or scope of those changes, Russian policy must change too. And for that change to occur, we have to create appropriate external circumstances and pressures. While reassuring Russia that its security is not presently at risk, we must nevertheless appraise Russia of the risks from continuing to try and intimidate Europe and restore an empire in violation of the 1989-91 status quo solemnized by several treaties, including those on arms control.

As long as it is not a democracy and is an international law-breaker, Russia cannot expect to be acknowledged as a true member of the G-8, or any democratic club, nor as a great power, certainly not a great European power. Neither can it be exempted from what is now the common practice whereby all governments' internal policies are subjected to constant foreign scrutiny. And Russia, based on its record, certainly cannot be entrusted with an exclusive sphere of interest around its peripheries based on "security zones" when it is a prime fomenter of regional instability. Indeed, such policies only ensure the ultimate crash of the present Russian status quo.

Therefore, simultaneously, robust engagement on arms control and pressure for democratization and respect for its neighbors' sovereignty, integrity, and independence must not only continue, but should grow and be regularly invoked by U.S. leaders precisely because Russia and other Eurasian governments have signed all these treaties, going back to the Helsinki treaty of 1975. The cornerstone of our demand for this kind of policy is the basic building block of world order, namely the doctrine of *Pacta Sunt Servanda* (treaties must be obeyed). And the conditions that gave rise to those treaties with regard to democratization in Europe have not been fully overcome, as Russian and Belarusian policy illustrate. Like it or not, Russia or its potential satellites cannot pretend successfully that they are being confronted with double standards or talk about Russia being a sovereign democracy as it now does. The treaties now in effect clearly outline a diminution of unbridled sovereignty and arguably any recognized international treaty does so too. That argument should be the cornerstone of our demands to treaty signatories, coupled with meaningful sanctions, not just economic, for failure to uphold these treaties.

Of course, there are also equally good security or strategic reasons for upholding democratization at every turn even as we seek avenues for negotiation. It is not just because we believe, with considerable justification, that states who reach democracy are ultimately stronger, even if they have to cross through dangerous waters to get there, it is also that, as noted above, Russia shows no sign of accepting responsibility for its actions and their consequences, e.g., in the frozen conflicts in Moldova, Georgia, or in Ukraine, let alone in its support for the repressive regimes of Central Asia or its arms sales abroad. To the extent that violence, crime, and authoritarian rule flourish in these states, they are all at risk of upheaval, even sudden upheaval as we have seen in Georgia, Kyrgyzstan, and Ukraine and in the repeated manifestations of internal violence that shook Uzbekistan in 2004-05 and could easily do so again. Such violence and instability could easily spread to Russia, as the example of Chechnya and the North Caucasus suggests.

Not pushing for reform even as we seek these states' security from attack by terrorists or from their incorporation in a Russian sphere of influence avails us little. For, as Tesmur Basilia, special assistant for economic issues to former Georgian President Edvard Shevarnadze, wrote, in many CIS countries, e.g., Georgia and Ukraine, "the acute issue of choosing between alignment with Russia and the West is associated with the choice between two models of social development."[329] Indeed, even some Russian analysts acknowledge the accuracy of this insight. Thus Dmitry Furman writes that, "The Russia-West struggle in the CIS is a struggle between two irreconcilable systems."[330] Furman even accepts the repressiveness of the current regime, saying that "Managed democracies are actually a soft variant of the Soviet system."[331]

The aptness of these observations transcends

Georgia and Ukraine to embrace the entire post-Soviet region, since it is clear that Moscow opposes "exporting democracy" to it. Indeed, it regards the idea with contempt and thus attracts the local dictators who cleave to it for support against Western pressures for democratization.[332] Basilia also pointed to the local perception of Russia as security threat.

> Nowadays there are many in the West who believe that Russia has changed and, having reformed, seeks to interact with neighboring countries in conformity with international norms. Some Eurasian countries would disagree with this opinion, and believe instead that the Russian mentality has not changed much, and that Russia continues to deem the "near abroad" as its sphere of social influence. After the second war with Chechnya, many think that Russia regards violence as its major tool for resolving social and political problems, especially with regard to non-Russian peoples from the former empire. Thus integration into the international community should be viewed as a guarantee for security and further development.[333]

The current silence or relative silence on democratic issues facilitates the exportation of Russia's sphere of influence and style of rule throughout the CIS, while strengthening Georgian, Ukrainian, and other democracies not only forestalls chances for internal upheaval in those states, it also rebuffs Russian imperialism and thus helps strengthen domestic Russian calls for reform. More urgently, it reduces Russia's chances to engineer long-standing reversals of both Westernization and democratization in Ukraine and elsewhere, outcomes that only reduce security throughout the CIS.

The logic is the same as George Kennan's even if containment is not the policy choice here. By standing on the basis of international law and the democratic choice of those states' peoples, not our own unilateral and hegemonic power, and by working intensively with those states who wish the benefits of association with the West, we can create examples of progress that will resonate in Russia and elsewhere while checking the spread of deformations of governance that only add to Russia's and our own insecurity. NATO was and is correct in observing that its and the EU's expansions enlarge the domain of security in Europe and Eurasia to the benefit of Russia, if not that of its elite, which can only survive by imperialism and predation.

Ultimately, then, the tenacious, insistent, and unceasing proclamation of deviations by Russia from its own promised course of action are legally and strategically strongly founded and mutually invigorating. A strategy that engages not only Russia on its vital issues and agenda, but also the CIS and Eastern Europe **on an equal basis with Russia** and does so while unceasingly proclaiming that democratic values enshrined in treaties must be upheld, benefits everyone except Russia's rulers. But it certainly redounds to the benefit of the long-suffering Russian people.[334] Neither does it represent an effort to overthrow Russia unless one wants to accept at face value the self-serving *pronunciamentos* of the ruling group. What must be understood as a guiding strategic principle here is that Russian autocracy and its corollary, Russian imperialism, are the gravest security threat facing Eurasia (including Europe and Russia itself) and are ultimately incompatible with any progress of the Russian people, or Eurasia to security, liberty, and prosperity.

A recent article by Danish scholar Sten Rynning insightfully cites the work of Lassa Oppenheim, the founder of the school of positive law, on these points. As Rynning writes, Oppenheim argued that, "International law can operate only under certain conditions, the two most important of which are *a balance of power and a shared conception of politics.*"[335] (Italics in the original.) Rynning further argues that the supply of WMD will be the focal point where these two conditions are met because "a shared conception of power within a working balance of power makes for satisfied or conservative great powers." These powers are uniquely empowered because of their size and reach to control the flow of the resources needed for WMD in the international system. And during the Cold War, the Nonproliferation Treaty (NPT) came into being exactly when they both became fully conscious of their mutual interest in controlling nuclear weapons.[336] The ensuing regime was supposed to bolster mutual deterrence, but it also enhanced bilateral communication and restricted nuclear weapons diffusion to other members of their alliance systems that helped counter the outbreak of new threats.[337]

However, today's world is rather different. Even if America has lost ground under the Bush administration, it still remains by far the greatest power and master of the strongest global alliance system. Thus a fundamental asymmetry or imbalance of power exists. Yet Washington cannot simply insist upon its demands and get its way, as current proliferation crises show us. Under the circumstances, we can either follow the logic of imbalance or strive to uphold the old balance in unfamiliar environments. As Rynning observes,

> If none of Oppenheim's conditions are met, if power is asymmetrically distributed and ideological conflict predominates, we encounter cases of *revisionist demand*; revisionists demand nuclear weapons as deliberate

instruments of expansion, because they wish to check hegemonic power and enhance the scope for their own values and desires. What happens when an order designed to control supply and counter misguided demand—by nature a generalized, universal order—encounters cases of revisionist demand? Gerry Simpson is in no doubt: legalized hegemony and anti-pluralism will move to the forefront of the international debate. Legalized hegemony denotes the hegemon's attempt to secure for itself special privileges justified on the grounds that it is policing the order; anti-pluralism denoted the political effort to delineate the ideas and ambitions that will earn some states the title of "outlaw" and cause their exclusion from the society of nations. The implication is that status quo powers cannot merely uphold the old order. They can either seek to *reshape* the old order to make it relevant and sustainable or they can more simply, but also dramatically seek to *replace* it with something new.[338] (Italics in the original)

Washington, in this case the hegemon, has sought by unilateral and multilateral actions (UN resolution 1540 and the Proliferation Security Initiative) to reshape that nuclear order. The multilateral moves have succeeded and are now part of international practice and law, whereas the unilateral moves to replace the old order, preemptive invasion of Iraq and a unilateral nuclear policy, have failed conspicuously to advance U.S. interests and nuclear security.[339] The U.S. nuclear weapons policy and overall nuclear unilateralism have stimulated Sino-Russian fears of U.S. intentions and capabilities as well as considerable criticism abroad of Washington's supposedly cavalier attitude towards arms control treaties.[340] Indeed, not only are North Korea and Iran examples of revisionist demand, so too is Russia, given its strong opposition to U.S. nuclear weapons policies, missile defenses, and nonproliferation policy. There is good reason to see in Russian policy for the last several years a move towards the revisionist demand posture that "demands nuclear weapons as deliberate instruments of expansion, because it wishes to check hegemonic power and enhance the scope for its own values and desires."[341]

This conjuncture of all these nuclear issues is not accidental. As Stephen Cimbala writes,

> The possible emergence of a nuclear armed Iran shows how the issue of cooperative security in Europe and the Middle East is directly linked to the U.S.-Russian problem of post-Cold War nuclear stability. Russian political support is necessary inside and outside of the UN Security Council in order to contain Iranian nuclear ambitions. To obtain this cooperation, the U.S. must reassure Russia that it has no interest in nuclear superiority with the intent of coercing Russia or using NATO as a vehicle for undermining the Russian regime. Missile defense, if deployed cannot have their Cold War flavor of competition for nuclear superiority, but must emerge from an environment of U.S.-Russian security cooperation.[342]

However, we are far away from that environment. Precisely because a state constituted as Russia now represents a standing invitation to uncontrolled military adventurism—of which there has been much in Russia's brief history and not least due to the absence of democratic control over the power ministries—it has to be checked.[343] There is no contradiction between engaging Russia on the great issues of proliferation and arms control and cooperating with it against the common enemy of terrorism, and at the same time insisting on its behaving according to European norms that it has accepted in the treaties it has signed, all with a view to integrating it with its European neighbors.

While this is certainly difficult in practice, it is hardly less difficult than the policy we now are conducting, which has left us attacked by unending crises with few if any governments willing to help us.

In fact, a policy that bases itself on treaties and laws rather than upon unilateral assertions of power is actually more effective than that alternative, even if it means narrowing the scope of freedom of action for unilateral American ventures.[344] As Robert Wright's recent argument for reforming U.S. foreign policy in general towards what he calls progressive realism contends,

> There is principle here that goes beyond arms control: the national interest can be served by constraints on American behavior when they constrain other nations as well. This logic covers the spectrum of international governance, from global warming, (we'll cut carbon dioxide emissions if you will) to war (we'll refrain from it if you will).[345]

Indeed, democratization is essential, first of all in regard to Russia's power agencies. The armed forces still regard NATO and the United States as their main enemies, and their exercises confirm it even to the point of often involving missile and nuclear strikes or large-scale conventional exercises against alleged terrorists. Second, although Putin, Medvedev, and Ivanov have endeavored to restructure at least some of the armed forces to fight primarily against terrorist attacks, which are the current main threat to Russian security, this use of the military in a counterterrorist or counterintelligence force can have the most serious negative domestic outcomes, as we have seen in Chechnya. Moreover, these forces could also easily be used as Gorbachev and Yeltsin had sought to use them, i.e., against democratic reform at home.[346] The more recent military buildup and emphasis on nuclear and anti-American scenarios within a framework of the presupposition of conflict will inevitably recreate pressures akin to those of the Cold War for military buildup because deterrence, while possibly restraining both sides from war, freezes them in a posture of global hostility across the global security agenda and stabilizes the rule of autocrats and great power chauvinists in Russia.

Third, the tendency to adventurism that led Moscow into its so-called peacemaking operations in the Caucasus and Moldova have now embroiled it in situations where the threat of war, particularly with Georgia, is constant and where Russian policy seems mainly to consist of provocations of Tbilisi to get it to launch a violent conflict or of responses to Tbilisi's own penchant for provocative acts.[347] So dangerous a policy inevitably has unforeseen consequences. The recent signs of military adventurism, buzzing Scotland, flights to Guam and the resumption of long-range air patrols, submarine races to plant the flag of sovereignty in the Arctic, and exercises with Venezuela in the Caribbean only serve the armed forces' myopic interest of "walking tall." They do nothing to enhance Russian security. And, finally, the lack of democratic control over the armed forces has been a constant and lethal aspect of Russian policy toward Chechnya which has resulted in frightful violations of human rights and which has generated in response a running series of low-intensity conflicts across the North Caucasus for which Moscow has no solution.

While democracy is not a panacea, it is safe to say that a democratically controlled military would have behaved differently as would its masters also have done. Indeed, it is arguable that what Russia's military fears most about NATO expansion is that it generates an external pressure that is supported by domestic reformers to democratize the entire range of Russian national security policy and subject it to civilian and democratic accountability under law, something that is anathema to that military-political elite.[348] Thus, ultimately there are compelling geostrategic reasons why the vigorous and ongoing insistence on reforms as signed in international treaties is an essential and indispensable part of any sound Western policy toward Russia.

While the next administration should take account of Russia's (and China's) interests, it cannot be bound and shackled by them. Those interests and the proposals emanating now from Moscow offer the next administration the opportunity to forge a strategy based upon cooperative engagement in arms control and to move forward to effect a mutually beneficial reshaping of the current status quo. At the same time, those arms control proposals that we are recommending for the next administration should be seen and included as part of a comprehensive strategy towards Russia that strives to reduce Russian opportunities for intimidating its neighbors and breaking free of international restraints even as we assume them upon ourselves. These proposals and the larger strategy within which it is embedded offer opportunities for both Russian security partnerships and a decline of tension throughout Eurasia that is a necessary prerequisite for further progress towards both peace and democratization.

If Moscow prefers conflict and the fantasy of neo-imperial revanche based upon deterrence and enduring great power hostility, we are not strong enough to reshape Eurasia unilaterally and simply exclude it as we move forward. That strategy was tried and failed, leaving us with a renewed entrapment in the mire of deterrence. We can maintain peace and possibly make limited advances towards our objectives in this fashion. But we do so at the cost of permanent tension, and Russia does so at the cost of setting the stage for what will likely be another political upheaval in its long history of aborted chances for peace and reform.

Despite the current seeming impasse in bilateral relations, there are opportunities for us in Russia's new arms control proposals, whatever their underlying intentions may be. We can either ignore them and move along the same unsatisfying lines that we have taken in the last 8 years, or we can exploit this opportunity and devise proposals that move us, Russia, and other key players farther in the direction of mutual security and peace than ever before. That outcome would be the most beneficial for all concerned. But Russia, too, has a choice; it can saddle itself with the continuation of the status quo because it is governed by suspicion, an egotism borne of the dizziness from success induced by oil and gas revenues and the neo-imperial dynamic inherent in autocracy. Or else Russia can choose to recover its professed European vocation and begin to deliver on the promise of prosperity, peace, and freedom for its citizens. Ultimately arms control issues are inseparable from the nature of the domestic regime in each country. Our regime will of necessity change in January 2009. And as the strongest player in the game and a truly "system-forming" power, it is up to us to take a leadership role in moving toward a new nuclear and overall order. But can Russia do so? Does it want to do so? Its formal proposals, no matter how they were intended, offer the next administration the opportunity not only to fulfill America's responsibilities both for and to the world, but also to help Russia begin to unchain itself from the fantasies and nightmares of the past. We can only hope that both Washington and Moscow seize those opportunities that now beckon to them.

ENDNOTES

1. "U.S. Demands Russia Leave Georgia 'Now'," *Reuters* and *the New York Times*, August 21, 2008; "U.S. Weighs Sanctions, Russia Nuclear Deal at Risk," *Reuters*, August 28, 2008; Jay Solomon and Gregory L. White, "U.S. Weighs Halt to Talks With Russia On Nuclear Arms Curbs," *Wall Street* Journal, August 29, 2008, p. A1.

2. Moscow, *Interfax*, in English, September 11, 2008, Open Source Committee, Foreign *Broadcast Information Service Central Eurasia* (henceforth *FBIS SOV*), September 11, 2008.

3. "Lugar, Nunn Warn of Danger to CTR Program," *Global Security Newswire*, September 18, 2008, *www.nti.org/d_newswire/issues/2008_9_18.html*.

4. "Russia Wants to Negotiate Arms Control with Obama," *Associated Press*, December 17, 2008.

5. Thom Shanker and Nicholas Kulish, "U.S. and Poland Set Nuclear Deal," *New York Times*, August 15, 2008, *www.nytimes.com;*" Jan Cienski and Andrew Ward, "Russia Warns Poland Over Missile Shield," *Financial Times*, August 15, 2008, *www.ft.com;* "Russia to 'Neutralize' US Missile Defense Threat," *Agence France Presse*, July 14, 2008.

6. "Ukraine Ready To Work With West on Missile Defense," *Radio Free Europe Radio Liberty*, August 16, 2008.

7. "Bildt Plays Down Russian Nuclear Threat," *The Local*, August 18, 2008," *www.thelocal.se/13780/20080818;* Mark Franchetti, "Russia's New Nuclear Challenge to Europe," *Timesonline*, August 17, 2008, *www.timesonline.co.uk/tol/news/worldeurope/article4547883.ece.*

8. "Russian Military Chief Defends Nonstrategic Nukes," *Global Security Newswire*, December 17, 2008, *gsn.nti.org*.

9. *Ibid.;* "Russia Orders 70 Nuclear Missiles by 2011; Report," *defensenews.com* from *Agence-France Presse*, December 22, 2008.

10. "Russia To Allocate $35.3 Billion For Arms Production in 2009-11," *RIA Novosti*, December 12, 2008; "Russian Military Confirms 13 Strategic Missile Launches for 2009," *RIA Novosti*, December 12, 2008.

11. "Oleg Shchedrov," "Russia To Axe Some Weapons If U.S. Abandons Shield," *Reuters*, December 19, 2008.

12. General of the Army Yuri N. Baluyevsky, "About the United States: What's Next? Who Needs a Missile Defense Umbrella and Why?" Moscow, *Voyenno-Promyshlennyi Kuryer*, in Russian, July 26, 2006, *FBIS SOV; Transcript of the Interactive Webcast of Press Conference With the President of Russia*, July 6, 2006, *www. Kremlin.ru.*

13. Stephen J. Cimbala, *The New Nuclear Disorder*, Unpublished Manuscript, forthcoming, pp. 1-3.

14. United States and Russian Federation, *U.S.-Russia Strategic Framework Declaration*, Washington, DC: The White House, Office of the Press Secretary, April 6, 2008; Cimbala, Vol. III, pp. 3, 7.

15. Remarks by the President to Students and Faculty at National Defense University, Fort Lesley J. McNair, May 1, 2001, *www.whitehouse.gov/news/releases/2001/05/20010501-10.html*.

16. Thomas Gomart, *EU-Russia Relations: Towards a Way Out of Depression, www.ifri.org*, 2008.

17. Colin Gray, *House of Cards*, Ithaca, NY: Cornell University Press, 1991; Keith Payne, *Deterrence In the Second Nuclear Age*, Lexington: University Press of Kentucky, 1996; Keith Payne; *Fallacies of Cold War Deterrence and a New Direction*, Lexington: University Press of Kentucky, 2001; Alexei Arbatov and General (Ret) Vladimir Dvorkin, *Beyond Nuclear Deterrence: Transforming*

the U.S.-Russian Equation, Washington, DC: Carnegie Endowment for International Peace, 2006, John F. Steinbruner, Foreword.

18. Patrick M. Morgan, *Deterrence Now*, Cambridge: Cambridge University Press, 2003, pp. 26-32.

19. *Ibid.*, p. 66.

20. Moscow, *Agentstvo Voyennykh Novostey Internet Version*, in Russian, September 10, 2008, *FBIS SOV*, September 10, 2008.

21. *Ibid.*

22. Open Source Committee, *OSC Analysis*, August 1, 2008, *FBIS SOV*, August 4, 2008.

23. Martin Sieff, "Russians Bet On Dems' Passion For Arms Control," *www.upi.com*, December 19, 2008; "US Sen Lugar Hopeful On Renewing Russia Nuclear Arms Treaty," *Agence France-Presse*, December 19, 2008, give the two conflicting impressions as to whether or not Russia is tying those missile defenses to achievement of a strategic nuclear missile treaty.

24. Moscow, *ITAR-TASS* in English, September 11, 2008, *FBIS SOV*, September 11, 2008.

25. Moscow, *Zvezda Television*, in Russian, September 11, 2008, *FBIS SOV*, September 11, 2008.

26. "Interview With Russian Foreign Minister Sergei Lavrov, Warsaw, *Gazeta Wyborcza*, September 11, 2008, and Moscow, *Ministry of Foreign Affairs Internet Version*, in English, September 15, 2008, *FBIS SOV*, September 15, 2008.

27. *Ibid.*

28. Dmitri Solovyov, "Russia Says It Must Have Nuclear Parity With U.S.," *Reuters*, December 7, 2007; Moscow, *Interfax*, in English, October 1, 2004, *FBIS SOV*, October 1, 2004.

29. Philip. P. Pan, "Russia Says U.S. Seeks Weaker Treaty: Landmark START I Nuclear Arms Control Agreement Set To

Expire Next Year," *washingtonpost.com*, December 20, 2008; Walter Pincus, "U.S., Russia Split Over Scope of Arms Treaty: Follow-Up But Concur On Goal, Negotiator Says," *washingtonpost.com*, December 22, 2008.

30. Ambassador Linton F. Brooks, *Arms Control and U.S.-Russian Relations*, Presentation to the Strategic Studies Institute Annual Strategy Conference: "US and Russia: Post-Elections Security Challenges," U.S. Army War College, Carlisle Barracks, PA, March 6-7, 2008.

31. Andrei Shumikhin, "Moscow's Debates On the Future Of Russia's Strategic Nuclear Forces," *National Institute For Public Policy*, Fairfax, VA, 1994, p. 3.

32. *Aktual'nye Zadachi Razvitie Vooruzhennykh Sil' Rossiiskoi Federatsii* (henceforth *Aktual'nye Zadachi*), Moscow, 2003, *www.mil. ru*; Keynote Address- HE Mr. Sergei Ivanov Minister of Defense of the Russian Federation, International Institute of Strategic Studies, London, July 13, 2004, *www.iiss.org/conference.php?confID=67*, accessed on May 11, 2005.

33. Pavel Podvig, "Russia and the Military Uses of Space," Pavel Podvig and Hui Zhang, eds., *Russian and Chinese Responses to U.S. Military Plans in Space*, Cambridge, MA: American Academy of Arts and Sciences, 2008, p. 2.

34. Alexander G. Savelyev, "Russian Defense and Arms Control Policy and Its Prospects After the Presidential Elections," *Unisci Discussion Papers*, No. 17, May, 2008, p. 105; Alexei G. Arbatov, *Russia and the United States – Time To End the Strategic Deadlock,* Briefing Paper, Carnegie Endowment for International Peace, Carnegie Moscow Center, Vol. X, No. 3, 2008, p. 2.

35. Alexei Arbatov, *Reducing the Role of Nuclear Weapons*, Paper Presented to the Conference on Achieving the Vision of a World Free of Nuclear Weapons, Oslo, February 26-27, 2008, pp. 5-6.

36. Moscow, *ITAR-TASS*, in English, September 29, 2008, *FBIS SOV*, September 29, 2008; Moscow, *Interfax*, in English September 29, 2008, *FBIS SOV*, September 29, 2008; Moscow, *Kommersant.com*, in English, September 30, 2008, *FBIS SOV*, September 30, 2008.

37. Bradley A. Thayer and Thomas M. Skypek, "Russia Goes Ballistic," *The National Interest*, September-October, 2008, pp. 61-68; Kurt R. Guthe, "A Different Path to Nuclear Arms Reductions," *Comparative Strategy*, Vol. XXVII, No. 4, 2008, pp. 332-335; Thomas Scheber, "Conventionally-Armed ICBMs: Time For Another Look," *Comparative Strategy*, Vol. XXVII, No. 4, 2008, pp. 336-344; Mark Schneider, "The Future of the U.S. Nuclear Deterrent," *Comparative Strategy*, Vol. XXVII, No. 4, 2008, pp. 345-360.

38. For example, Morgan, p. 10.

39. Stephen Blank, *Towards a New Russia Policy,* Carlisle, PA: Strategic Studies Institute, U.S. Army War College, 2008.

40. *Aktual'nye Zadachi,* July, 15, 2008, *www.kremlin.ru*, available from *FBIS SOV* July 17, 2008; Stephen Blank, "Threats to and from Russia: An Assessment," *Journal of Slavic Military Studies*, forthcoming; Jacob Kipp, "Russia: New Draft Military Doctrine," Ustina Markus and Daniel N. Nelson, eds., *Brassey's Eurasian and East European Security Yearbook*, Washington, DC: Brassey's, 2000, p. 343.

41. Lieutenant General V. A. Gusachenko, "Ob Aktual'nom Kontekste Ponyatiya "Natisonal'naya Bezopastnosti," *Voyennaya Mysl'*, No. 7, 2007, p. 2.

42. *FBIS SOV*, September 10, 2008.

43. *Ibid.*

44. Moscow, *Agentstvo Voyennykh Novostey Internet Version*, in English, September 29, 2008, *FBIS SOV,* September 29, 2008.

45. Blank, "Threats to and from Russia."

46. "Interview with Foreign Minister Sergei Lavrov," *Rossiyskaya Gazeta*, February 21-28, 2007, *www.mid.ru*.

47. Arbatov, *Russia and the United States – Time To End the Strategic Deadlock*, p. 2.

48. We should remember that of the 21 people brought in to discuss Russia's response to American calls for support after 9/11, 18 opposed support for American military presence in Central Asia, 2 abstained, and Putin was alone.

49. Blank, "The Unending Crisis of Russian Defense Industry."

50. Thayer and Skypek, pp. 61-68; Guthe, pp. 332-335; Scheber, pp. 336-344; Schneider, pp. 345-360; Adrian Bloomfield, "Russia To Build Eight Nuclear Submarines," *Daily Telegraph,* October 3, 2008.

51. "Russia Flexes Its Military Muscle with Missile Launches," *The Australian,* October 13, 2008.

52. Remarks by Stephen Blank, Eugene Rumer, Mikhail Tsypkin, and Alexander Golts at the Heritage Foundation Program, "The Russian Military: Modernization and the Future," April 8, 2008, *www.heritage.org/press/events/ev040808a.cfm;* Stephen Blank, "The Political Economy of the Russian Defense Sector," Jan Leijhonhielm and Frederik Westerlund, eds., *Russian Power Structures: Present and Future Roles in Russian Politics,* Stockholm: Swedish Defense Research Agency, 2008, pp. 97-128.

53. Vadim Solovyev, "Our General Staff Responds to NATO," Moscow, *Nezavisimoye Voyennoye Obozreniye,* in Russian, January 24, 2003, *FBIS SOV,* January 24, 2003; Vladimir Ivanov, "Concern With Subsequent Satisfaction: Minister of Defense Sergey Ivanov Promised That Russia Will Not Conduct Preventive Nuclear Strikes," Moscow, *Nezavisimoye Voyennoye Obozreniye,* in Russian, October 17, 2003, *FBIS SOV,* October 17, 2003; *Aktual'nye Zadachi.*

54. Alexander Avdeyev, "Russia—Reliable Friend of Yugoslavia," *Review of International Affairs* (Belgrade), 1999, p. 24.

55. Sergei Kortunov, "Beyond Deterrence," Moscow, *Intelligent.ru,* in Russian, August 11, 2006, *FBIS SOV,* August 11, 2006.

56. "Putin Interviewed by Journalists from G8 countries—text," *www.kremlin.ru,* June 4, 2007.

57. For example, the Interview with Lavrov, Moscow, *Zvezda Television*, in Russian, September 11, 2008, *FBIS SOV*, September 11, 2008.

58. Pavel Podvig, *Revolution in Military Affairs: Challenges to Russia's Security,"* Paper Presented at the VTT Energy Styx Seminar, Helsinki, Finland, September 4, 2001, *www.armsocntol. ru/Podvig/eng/publications/misc/20010904styx.shtm.*

59. "Pentagon Sees Russia Strengthening Nuclear Deterrent," *Reuters*, June 9, 2008.

60. Elaine M. Grossman, "U.S. Navy Eyes Rising Need To Defend Czechs, Poles," *Global Security Newswire*, August 1, 2008, *www.nti.org.*

61. Vice Admiral Sandy Winnefield, "Maritime Strategy in an Age of Blood and Belief," *Proceedings of the U.S. Naval Institute,* July, 2008, p. 22.

62. *Ibid.*, p. 33.

63. "Robert Gates Says Russia Makes USA Increase its Nuclear Potential," *www.pravda.ru*, June 10, 2008.

64. "Interview with Foreign Minister Sergei Lavrov," *Rossiyskaya Gazeta*, February 21-28, 2007, *www.mid.ru.*

65. Moscow, *ITAR-TASS*, in English, June 20, 2008, *FBIS SOV*, June 20, 2008.

66. Moscow, *Interfax*, in English, July 7, 2008, *FBIS SOV*, July 7, 2008.

67. Kontseptsiya; *FBIS SOV*, July 17, 2008.

68. Speech at a Meeting With German Political, Parliamentary, and Civic Leaders, Berlin, June 5, 2008, *www.kremlin.ru/eng/ speeches/2008/06/05/2203_type82912type82914type84779_202153. shtml.*

69. Moscow, *Interfax*, in English, July 8, 2008, *FBIS SOV*, July 8, 2008.

70. U.S. Department of Defense, Nuclear Posture Review (henceforth NPR), *www.defenselink.mil/news/Jan2002/d20020109npr.pdf*; Kerry M. Kartcher, "U.S. Nuclear Weapons and Nonproliferation: Dispelling the Myths," Presentation to the Carnegie Moscow Center, February 2, 2007, available at *www.carnegie.ru/en/pubs/media/101192007.02.02.Presentation.ppt*.

71. Kartcher, *Ibid.*

72. Stephen Blank, "Undeterred: The Return of Nuclear War," *Georgetown Journal of International Affairs*, Vol. I, No. 2, Summer/Fall 2000, pp. 55-63; China's test of an anti-satellite weapon (ASAT) in January 2007 is only the latest manifestation of these trends to weaponize space.

73. Brooks.

74. Savelyev, p. 101.

75. Dennis M. Gormley, *Missile Contagion: Cruise Missile Proliferation and the Threat to International Security*, Westport, CT: Praeger Security International, 2008, pp. 175-176.

76. Gray.

77. Gormley.

78. F. Stephen Larrabee, "Whither Missile Defense?" *The International Spectator*, Vol. XLIII, No. 2, June 2008, pp. 5-13.

79. *Ibid.*

80. David S. McDonough, "Nuclear Superiority: The 'New Triad' and the Evolution of Nuclear Strategy," *Adelphi Paper* No. 383, 2006; Keir A. Lieber and Daryl G. Press, "The Rise of U.S. Nuclear Primacy," *Foreign Affairs*, Vol. LXXXV, No. 2, March-April, 2006, pp. 42-54; Keir A. Lieber and Daryl G. Press, "The End of MAD: The Nuclear Dimensions of U.S. Primacy," *International Security*, Vol. XX, No. 4, Spring 2006, pp. 7-44; George Bunn and

Christopher F. Chyba, eds., *U.S. Nuclear Policy: Confronting Today's Threats*, Foreword, William J. Perry, Washington, DC: Brookings Institution Press, 2006.

81. David McDonough, "The US Nuclear Shift to the Pacific," *RUSI Journal*, April, 2006, pp. 64-68.

82. *2007 South Carolina Democratic primary debate*, on MSNBC April 26, 2007, *www.issues2000.org/Archive/2007_Dem_primary_SC_Joe_Biden.htm*.

83. *Report of the Defense Science Board Task Force on Nuclear Capabilities: Report Summary*, Office of the Under Secretary of Defense for Acquisition, Technology, and Logistics, Washington, DC, December, 2006, pp. 11-12.

84. *Ibid.*, pp. 12-13.

85. *Ibid.*

86. "US Report Warns of Russian Nuclear Threat," *Jane's Intelligence Digest*, January 26, 2007, *jid.janes.com*.

87. Thayer and Skypek, pp. 61-68; Guthe, pp. 332-335; Scheber, pp. 336-344; Schneider, pp. 345-360.

88. Thayer and Skypek, p. 68.

89. Igor Plugtarev and Viktor Myasnikov, "Vice Prime Minister Sergey Ivanov, Governors, and Twenty thousand Soldiers," Moscow, *Nezavisimoye Voyennoye Obozreniye*, in Russian, September 29, 2006, *FBIS SOV*, October 4, 2006.

90. *Aktual'nye Zadachi.*

91. Open Source Committee, *OSC Analysis*, August 1, 2008, *FBIS SOV*, August 4, 2008, Open Source Committee, *OSC Analysis*, August 1, 2008, *FBIS SOV*, August 4, 2008.

92. Lieber and Press, "The Rise of U.S. Nuclear Primacy," pp. 42-54; Lieber and Press, "The End of MAD?: The Nuclear Dimensions of U.S. Primacy," pp. 7-44.

93. McDonough, "The US Nuclear Shift to the Pacific," *p.* 68.

94. Vladimir Dvorkin, *The Russian Debate on the Nonproliferation of Weapons of Mass Destruction and Delivery Vehicles*, Belfer Center for Science and International Affairs, Harvard University, Cambridge, MA. No. 4, 2004, p. 9.

95. Kartcher.

96. Elizabeth Bumiller, "McCain Vows To Work With Russia On Arms," *New York Times*, May 27, 2008, *ww2w.nytimes. com*; Barack Obama, "Towards a Nuclear Free World," *www. barackobama.com/issues/foreignpolicy/*, accessed on July 20, 2008.

97. Obama, "Towards a Nuclear Free World."

98. Paris, *AFP North European Service*, in English, September 11, 2008, *FBIS SOV*, September 11, 2008.

99. Sydney J. Freedberg, Jr., "Beyond Iraq," *National Journal*, July 12, 2008, *www.nationaljournal.com*.

100. Kontseptsiya; *FBIS SOV*, July 17, 2008.

101. *Ibid.*

102. For Medvedev's call for a sphere of influence, see "Interview Given By President Dmitry Medvedev to Television Channel One," Moscow, August 31, 2008, *www.kremlin.ru/eng/ speeches/2008/08/31/1850_type82912type82916_206003.shtml*.

103. Kontseptsiya; *FBIS SOV*, July 17, 2008.

104. *Ibid.*

105. Dmitri Trenin, "A Less Ideological America," *The Washington Quarterly*, Vol. XXXI, No. 4, Autumn, 2008, p. 119.

106. Kontseptsiya; *FBIS SOV*, July 17, 2008.

107. Michael H. Clemmesen's Weblog, "29/4/07: The Real RootsoftheTallinnMayhem," *blog.clemmesen.org/2007/04/29/28407-the mayhem-in-tallinn/*.

108. Robert Dalsjo, "Emerging Security Threats," Tommi Koivula and Jyrki Helminen, eds., *Armed Forces for Tomorrow*, Helsinki: National Defence University: Department of Strategic and Defence Studies, Series 2 Research Reports No. 39, 2007, pp. 22-23.

109. E-mail Letter from Darrell Hammer, *Johnson's Russia List*, February 5, 1997; Dmitry Trenin, "Transformation of Russian Foreign Policy: NATO Expansion Can Have Negative Consequences for the West," *Nezavisimaya Gazeta*, February 5, 1997, E-Mail Transmission; J. Michael Waller, "Primakov's Imperial Line," *Perspective*, Vol. VII, No. 3, January-February 1997, pp. 2-6; "Primakov, Setting a New, Tougher Foreign Policy," *Current Digest of the Post-Soviet Press* (henceforth *CDPP*), Vol. XLIX, No. 2, February 12, 1997, pp. 4-7.

110. Sergey M. Rogov, "Russia and NATO's Enlargement: The Search for a Compromise at the Helsinki Summit," Center for Naval Analyses, Alexandria, VA CIM 513/ May 1997, p. 10.

111. "Geopolitika i Russkaya Bezopasnost'," *Krasnaya Zvezda*, July 31, 1999, p. 2.

112. Dmitri Furman, "A Silent Cold War," *Russia in Global Affairs*, Vol. IV, No. 2, April-June, 2006, p. 73.

113. *Poslanie Federal'nomu Sobraniiu Rossiiskoi Federatsii*, April 26, 2007, *www.kremlin.ru/speeches/2007/04/26*; CFE Treaty on Verge of Collapse, Iran Threat Overblown-Russian Gen." *RIA Novosti*, May 10, 2007; Viktor Litovkin, "In the Language of Ultimatums," *Nezavisimaya Gazeta*, June 25, 2007, retrieved from *Johnson's Russia List*, JRL #2007-140, June 25, 2007.

114. "Moscow's Plan To Build Military Base in Moldova Rejected-Voronin," *Interfax*, October 30, 2005.

115. Vladimir Socor, "Russia Wants a Wholly Different Treaty on Conventional Forces in Europe," *Eurasia Daily Monitor*, June

13, 2007; Richard Weitz, "Georgia and the CFE Saga," *Central Asia Caucasus Analyst*, June 27, 2007, *www.cacianalyst.org/newsite*.

116. Information on the decree "On Suspending the Russian Federation's Participation in the Treaty on Conventional Armed Forces in Europe and Related International Agreements," July 14, 2007, w*ww.kremlin.ru/eng/text/docs/2007/07/137851.shtml*.

117. Socor, "Russia Wants a Wholly Different Treaty on Conventional Forces in Europe"; Weitz.

118. Vladimir Socor, "NATO Holds Firmly at Extraordinary CFE Conference With Russia," *Eurasia Daily Monitor*, June 18, 2007.

119. Moscow, *Agentstvo Voyennykh Novostey Internet Version*, in English, December 4, 2003, *FBIS SOV*, December 4, 2003.

120. Boris Volkonsky, "Cool War," *Kommersant*, June 27, 2007, Cited in *Transnistrian Digest*, No. 54, June 29, 2007.

121. Oleg Gorupay, "The South Caucasus," Moscow, *Kransaya Zvezda*, in Russian, October 18, 2006, *FBIS SOV*, October 18, 2006.

122. Weitz.

123. Vladimir Socor, "Gudauta Base and Unaccounted-For-Treaty-Limited Equipment: Ongoing Russian Breaches of CFE Treaty Commitments," *Eurasia Daily Monitor*, June 18, 2007.

124. Ivan Petrov, " Arms Race Near Our Border," *proUA,.com*, in Russian, June 6, 2008, *FBIS SOV*, July 21, 2008; Oleg Petrovsky, "Saakashvili: New Blood," Moscow, *Utro.ru, Internet Version*, in Russian, November 19, 2007, *FBIS SOV*, November 19, 2007.

125. Wade Bosese, "Russia Unflinching On CFE Treaty Suspension," *Arms Control Today*, May 2008, pp. 29-30; Wade Boese, "Georgian Conflict Clouds Future Arms Pacts," *Arms Control Today*, September 2008, pp. 33-34.

126. Curtis Harrington, "US Combat Aircraft Battle To Cover NATO Airspace," *Jane's Defence Weekly*, September 18, 2008, *jdw.janes.com*.

127. Julian E. Barnes and Paul Richter, "NATO Rapid-Response Unit Proposed to Address Fears About Russia," *Los Angeles Times*, September 19, 2008.

128. Moscow, *ITAR-TASS*, in English, September 12, 2008, *FBIS SOV*, September 12, 2008.

129. Guy Dinmore, Demetri Sevatopulo, and Hubert Wetzel; "Russia Confronted Rumsfeld With Threat to Quit Key Nuclear Treaty," *Financial Times*, March 9, 2005, p. 1.

130. "Scrapping Medium-Range Ballistic Missiles a Mistake-Ivanov-1," *RIA Novosti*, February 7, 2007.

131. Demetri Sevastopoulo, Neil Buckley, and Daniel Dombey, "Russia Threatens to Quit Arms Treaty," *Financial Times*, February 15, 2007, *www.ft.com*.

132. Vladimir Petrov, "Russia Releases Draft of Global INF Treaty," *Jane's Defence Weekly*, February 22, 2008, *ww4/janes.com/subscribe/jdw*.

133. Martin Sieff, "Russia Rattles Missile Treaty," *UPI*, March 2, 2006.

134. Luke Harding, "We Will Dump Nuclear Treaty, Putin Warns," *The Guardian*, October 13, 2007, *awww.guardian.co.uk/world/2007/oct/13/Russia.international*, accessed on July 23, 2008.

135. *Interfax*, February 27, 2006.

136. Sokov, p. 141.

137. Smith, p. 13.

138. "US Defense Chief Sees Problems in Russian Withdrawal from INF," *ITAR-TASS*, February 16, 2007.

139. "The ISCIP Analyst," Vol. XIII, No. 9, March 8, 2007, Boston, MA: Institute for the Study of Conflict, Ideology, and Policy, Boston University, *www.bu.edu/iscip*.

140. Gunnar Arbman and Charles Thornton, *Russia's Tactical and Nuclear Weapons Part I: Background and Policy Issues*, Stockholm, Swedish Defense Research Agency, 2003, *Part II: Technical Issues and Policy Recommendations*, Stockholm: Swedish Defense Research Agency, 2005.

141. Sergei Blagov, "Missiles for Kaliningrad," *ISN Security* watch, July 16, 2007, *www.isn.ethz.ch/news/sw/details. cfm?id=17863*.

142. "Moscow Says No Nuclear Weapons in Belarus to Counter U.S. Shield," *RIA Novosti*, August 6, 2008; "Russia Mulls Missiles in Belarus to Offset U.S.," *Washington Times*, August 7, 2008.

143. For example, *Ibid.*; Nikolai Poroskov, "A Nuclear Outpost," *Vremya Novostei*, July 7, 2004, *FBIS SOV*, July 7, 2004; Vladimir Socor, "Russia Warns of Missile-Forward Deployment in Kaliningrad Region," *Eurasia Daily Monitor*, July 6, 2007.

144. Nikolai Sokov, "'Tactical Nuclear Weapons' Scare of 2001," *CNS Reports*, January 4, 2001, *cns.miis.edu/pubs/reports/tnw. htm*.

145. Peter Baker, "U.S. and Russia to Enter Civilian Nuclear Pact,' *Washington Post*, July 8, 2006, p. A1.

146. Bumiller; Obama, "Towards a Nuclear Free World."

147. Gormley.

148. "Russia Revises Military Doctrine To Reflect Global Changes," *RIA Novosti*, March 6, 2007; "Russia's New Military Doctrine Declares USA and NATO Key Potential Enemies," *www. pravda.ru*, February 22, 2008.

149. Moscow, *Agentstvo Voyennykh Novostey Internet Version*, in English, February 8, 2008, *FBIS SOV*, February 8, 2008; Moscow, *ITAR-TASS*, in English, February 8, 2008, *FBIS SOV*, February 8, 2008.

150. Andrei Shoumikhin, *Russian Probes on Arms Control Regimes*, National Institute for Public Policy, 2005, pp. 6-9, *www. nipp.org*.

151. That would harmonize with Thayer Skypek's arguments as well. Thayer and Skypek, pp. 61-68.

152. Moscow, *Interfax, Agentstvo Voyennykh Novostey* March 17, 2005, *FBIS SOV*, March 17, 2005, cited in Shoumikhin, pp. 9-10.

153. Pavel Felgenhauer, "Russia Serious About INF Treaty Abrogation, " *Eurasia Daily Monitor*, February 21, 2007.

154 . Pavel Felgengauer, "The Syrian Advance," Moscow, *Novaya Gazeta*, in Russian, November 19, 2007, *FBIS SOV*, November 19, 2007.

155. Arbman and Thornton, Vol. II, p. 50; "Iskaner/SS-26," *www.globlasecurity.org*, accessed on July 24, 2008.

156. Nikolai Sokov, "Russia Tests a New Ground-Launched Cruise Missile and a New Strategic Missile On the Same Day," CNS Research Story, James Martin Center for Nonproliferation Studies, June 1, 2007, *cns.miis.edu/pubs/week/070601.htm*.

157. Alon Ben-David, "*Iskander*-E 'Designed To Counter Western TMDs'," *Jane's Defence Weekly*, April 6, 2005, *www4janes. com/subscribe/jdw/doc*.

158. *Ibid.*; Arbman and Thornton, Vol. II, p. 51.

159. "*Iskander/SS-26*"; Socor; Blagov.

160. Blagov.

161. Doug Richardson, "Russia Tests Cruise Missile for Islander TEL," *www.janes.com/news/defenceair/jr/*, June 8, 2007.

162. "Russia To Compensate For INF Losses With *Iskander* Missile System," *RIA Novosti*, November 15, 2007; "Russia to

Deploy *Iskander* Missiles in Three Years: Official," *Associated Press,* September 6, 2007.

163. Gormley, pp. 60, 68, 122.

164. Baker Spring, "Russian Withdrawal From the INF Treaty Will Put the Ball in Europe's Court," *Heritage Foundation Web Memo,* No. 1367, February 22, 2007, pp. 1-2.

165. Yantis A. Stivachtis, "The International System and the Use of Weapons of Mass Destruction," Eric Herring, ed., *Preventing the Use of Weapons of Mass Destruction,* London: Frank Cass Publishers, 2001, p. 104.

166. *Ibid.;* Solovyov, *FBIS SOV,* October 1, 2004.

167. Brad Roberts, "1995 and the End of the Post-Cold War Era," *Washington Quarterly,* Vol. XVIII, No. 1, retrieved from Lexis-Nexis.

168. Stivachtis, p. 105.

169. *Ibid.,* p. 127.

170. "Tactical Exercises Held To Prepare Strategic Aircraft for use in Regional Conflicts," *Nezavisimoye Voyennoye Obozreniye,* April 21, 2000, *BBC Summary of World Broadcasts,* May 3, 2000; Giles Whittell, "Russian Wargames To Test Missiles," *London Times,* February 16, 2001.

171. Stivachtis, p. 119.

172. Roberts.

173. Artem Troitsky, "Interview With CINC Ground Troops General of the Army Vladimir Anatolyevich Boldyrev," Moscow, *Voyenno-Promyshlennyi Kuryer,* in Russian, October 1, 2008, *FBIS SOV,* October 19, 2008.

174. Martin Nesirsky, "Russia Says Threshold Lower for Nuclear Weapons," *Reuters,* December 17, 1999.

175. Stephen Cimbala, *Shield of Dreams: Missile Defense and U.S.-Russian nuclear Strategy*, Annapolis, MD: U.S. Naval Institute, 2008.

176. See the essays in Brian Alexander and Alistair Millar, eds., *Tactical Nuclear Weapons: Emergent Threats In an Evolving Security Environment*, Stansfield Turner, Foreword, Washington, DC: Brassey's, 2003.

177. Arbman and Thornton, Vol. I, p. 11.

178. Alexander Yemelyanenkov, "Five Questions For the 'Five'," Moscow, *Rossiyskaya Gazeta*, in Russian, July 29, 2005, *FBIS SOV*, July 29, 2005; Schneider, p. 348.

179. *FBIS SOV*, July 7, 2004.

180. *Ibid.*

181. "Tactical Nuclear Weapons Can Be Allocated in Georgia and Ukraine," *www.regnum.ru/english/1063182.html*, October 1, 2008.

182. "Baltic Fleet To Climb Higher," Kaliningrad, *Kaliningradskaya Vecherka*, in Russian, September 11, 2008, *FBIS SOV*, September 11, 2008.

183. Franchetti.

184. Kaliningrad, *Kaliningradskaya Vecherka*, in Russian, September 11, 2008, *FBIS SOV*, September 11, 2008.

185. Arbman and Thornton, Vol. I, p. 35.

186. Paul I. Bernstein, John P. Caves, Jr., and John F. Reichart, *The Future Nuclear Landscape*, Washington, DC: Center for the Study of Weapons of Mass Destruction, National Defense University, Fort Lesley J. McNair, Occasional Papers No. 5, 2007, pp. 26-27.

187. "Putin Alarmed by US Nuke Policy," *The Russia Journal*, April 9, 2002, *www.russiajournal.ru/newsrj_news.shtml?nd=1931*; Moscow, *ITAR-TASS*, in Russian, July 4, 2006, *FBIS SOV*, July 4, 2006.

188. Schneider, p. 348.

189. Dmitry Kitovkin, "Terrorists Cannot Be Frightened With Nuclear Genie," Moscow, *Izvestiya*, in Russian, April 9, 2004, *FBIS SOV*, April 9, 2004.

190. *FBIS SOV*, July 7, 2004.

191. Ivan Safranchuk, "Tactical Nuclear Weapons in the Modern World: a Russian Perspective," in Alexander and Millar, eds., p. 54.

192. *Ibid.*, p. 66.

193. Nikolai Sokov, "The Russian Nuclear Arms Control Agenda After SORT," *Arms Control Today*, April, 2003, *www. armscontrol.org/act/2003/04sokovapro3.asp*.

194. Moscow, *ITAR-TASS, in Russian*, October 7, 2004, *FBIS SOV*, October 7, 2004, cited in Arbman and Thornton, Vol. II, p. 75.

195. Podvig, *Revolution in Military Affairs*; Arbman and Thornton, Vol. I, pp. 34-44.

196. Shumikhin, pp. 10-12.

197. Arbman and Thornton, Vol. II, p. 74.

198. Moscow, *ITAR-TASS*, in English, June 9, 2005, *FBIS SOV*, June 9, 2005.

199. Vladimir Isachenkov, "U.S. Diplomat: Russia Falls Short of Its Obligations to Reduce Tactical Nuclear Weapons," *Associated Press*, April 12, 2006; Yui Kotenok, "Russia Builds a Missile Defense Net," Moscow, *Utro.ru*, in Russian, June 4, 2007, *FBIS SOV*, June 4, 2007.

200. Eric Schmitt, "Up To 480 U.S. Nuclear Arms in Europe, Private Study Says," *New York Times*, February 9, 2005; "U.S. Actions and Policies In Support of Its NPT Article VI Obligations Related

to Nuclear Disarmament," *Fact Sheet, Bureau of Nonproliferation,* Washington, DC, May 1, 2003, *www.state.gov/t/isn/rls/fs/24918,htm,* accessed July 25, 2008.

201. Sokov, "The Russian Nuclear Arms Control Agenda."

202. *Ibid.*

203. Cimbala, Vol. V, pp. 22-23.

204. Arbman and Thornton, Vol. II, p. 2.

205. *FBIS SOV,* July 7, 2004; Vladimir Mukhin, "NATO Troops Occupied Minsk," Moscow, *Nezavisimoye Voyennoye Obozreniye,* in Russian, July 16, 2004, *FBIS SOV,* July 16, 2004.

206. Arbman and Thornton, Vol. I, pp. 37-38.

207. Moscow, *ITAR-TASS,* September 3, 2007, in *Johnson's Russia List,* September 3, 2007.

208. Conversations with Officials from the State Department, Carlisle Barracks, PA, July 22, 2008; Arbman and Thornton, Vol. I, pp. 44-48.

209. "Russia: the Significance of Missiles in Belarus," *www. stratfor.com/analysis,* July 30, 2008.

210. "Russia In Ukraine Missile Threat," *BBC News,* February 12, 2008, *news.bbc.co.uk/2hi/europe/7241470.stm;* Max Franchetti, "Europe Faces Russian Missile Threat," *TimesOnline.co.uk/tol/ news/world/Europe/article4322468,* July 13, 2008.

211. *FBIS SOV,* July 21, 2008; Alexander Mitrofanov, "Russia, Oil, and Missiles," Prague, *Pravo Outline,* in Czech, July 16, 2008, *FBIS SOV,* July 20, 2008; Alexander Alesin, "The Strategy Turns Out That It Could Be Even Worse," Minsk, *Belorusskiy Rynok,* in Russian, June 23, 2008, *FBIS SOV,* July 21, 2008.

212. "Russian Expert Says Missile Shield May Undermine Russian-Bulgarian Relations," Sofia, *BTA,* July 23, 2008.

213. Atlantic Council of the United States, *Restoring Georgia's Sovereignty in Abkhazia*, David L. Phillips, Project Director and Author, 2008, p. 17.

214. "Russia: A Military Response to U.S. BMD," *Stratfor Analysis, www.stratfor.com*, July 14, 2008.

215. "Russia, China Challenge US With Proposal To Ban Space Weapons At Disarmament Conference," *Associated Press, International Herald Tribune*, February 12, 2008, *www.iht.com/articles/ap/2008/02/12/bews/Disarmament-Space-Weapons.php*.

216. Podvig, "Russia and the Military Uses of Space," pp. 2-3; Podvig, *Challenges to Russia's Security,*" Lieutenant General G. P. Kuprianov (Ret), "Principal Trends in the Evolution Of Space Warfare," Moscow, *Voyennaya Mysl' (Military Thought)* in Russian, March 31, 2005, *FBIS SOV*, March 31, 2005.

217. Peter Raimov, "If War Will Come Tomorrow," Stephen J. Cimbala, ed., *The Russian Military Into the Twenty-First Century*, London: Frank Cass, 2001, p. 32.

218. *Ibid.*

219. "Russia Orders Upgrade of Nuclear Deterrent," *Radio Free Europe Radio Liberty*, September 26, 2008.

220. Moscow, *Agentstvo Voyennykh Novostey Internet Version*, in English, January 23, 2008, *FBIS SOV*, January 23, 2008.

221. Pavel Razgulayev, "Russia Is Losing to the USA," Moscow, *www.utro.ru Internet Version*, in Russian, January 21, 2008, *FBIS SOV*, January 21, 2008.

222. For example, Moscow, *ITAR-TASS*, in Russian, March 28, 2004, *FBIS SOV*, March 28, 2004; Moscow, *ITAR-TASS, in English*, March 4, 2004, *FBIS SOV*, March 4, 2004.

223. Baluyevsky, *FBIS SOV*, July 6, 2006.

224. *FBIS SOV*, September 15, 2008.

225. Kathryn L. Gauthier, "China as Peer Competitor? Trends in Nuclear Weapons, Space and Information Warfare," Lawrence E. Grinter, ed., *The Dragon Awakes: China's Military Modernization: Trends and Implications*, Maxwell AFB, AL: USAF Counterproliferation Center, 1999, pp. 25-34; Mark A. Stokes, *China's Strategic Modernization: Implications for the United States*: Carlisle, PA: Strategic Studies Institute, U.S. Army War College, 1999, pp. 96-109; David J. Smith, "Sun Tzu and the Modern Art of Countering Missile Defense," *Jane's Intelligence Review*, January 2000, pp. 35-39.

226. "Russia, China Challenge US."

227. Shumikhin, p. 12.

228. Peter Brookes, "Opinion: Marking the Boundaries of Weapon Use in Space," *Jane's Defence Weekly*, July 22, 2008.

229. *Ibid.*

230. "Russia Determined to Retaliate If Other Nations Deploy Weapons in Space," *www.pravda.ru*, September 27, 2007.

231. Shumikhin, pp. 12-15, *FBIS SOV*, March 31, 2005.

232. Moscow, *Agentstvo Voyennykh Novostey Internet Version*, in Russian, January 31, 2008, *FBIS SOV*, January 31, 2008.

233. Moscow, *Interfax-AVN Internet Version* in English, June 2, 2006, *FBIS SOV*, June 2, 2006.

234. Podvig, "Russia and the Military Uses of Space," pp. 25-29.

235. David Kerr, "The Sino-Russian Partnership and U.S. Policy Toward North Korea, "From Hegemony to Concert in Northeast Asia," *International Studies Quarterly*, Vol. XXXXIX, No. 3, September 2005, pp. 411-437; Constantine C. Menges, *China: The Gathering Threat*, Nashville, TN: Nelson Current Publishers, 2005; Stephen Blank, "Towards Alliance? The Strategic Implications of Russo-Chinese Relations," *National Security Studies Quarterly*, Vol. VII, No. 3, Summer, 2001, pp. 1-30.

236. Kerr, pp. 411-437.

237. Robert Jervis, "U.S. Grand Strategy: Mission Impossible," *Naval War College Review*, Summer 1998, pp. 22-36; Richard K. Betts, "Power, Prospects, and Priorities: Choices for Strategic Change," *Naval War College Review*, Winter 1997, pp. 9-22; John C. Gannon, "Intelligence Challenges Through 2015," *odci.gov/cia/ publicaffairs/speeches/gannon_speech_05022000.html.*

238. Menges.

239. *Ibid*; Kerr, pp. 411-437; Pei, p. 17.

240. Kim Yo'ng Hu'i, "The Relevance of Central Asia," Seoul, Korea, *JoongAng Ilbo Internet Version*, in English, July 11, 2005, *FBIS SOV*, July 11, 2005.

241. Lyle Goldstein and Vitaly Kozyrev, "China, Japan and the Scramble for Siberia," *Survival*, Vol. XLVIII, No. 1, Spring, 2006, pp. 175-176.

242. John J. Tkacik, Jr., "How the PLA Sees North Korea," Andrew Scobell and Larry M. Wortzel, eds., *Shaping China's Security Environment: The Role of the People's Liberation Army*, Carlisle, PA: Strategic Studies Institute, U.S. Army War College, 2006, pp. 160-163.

243. McDonough, "The US Nuclear Shift to the Pacific," pp. 64-68.

244. Jonathan Pollack, "U.S. Strategies in Asia: A Revisionist Hegemon," Byung-Kook Kim and Anthony Jones, eds., *Power and Security in Northeast Asia: Shifting Strategies*, Boulder, CO: Lynne Rienner Publishers, 2007, pp. 86-87.

245. Moscow, *Interfax, in English, October 24, 2007, FBIS SOV,* October 24, 2007.

246. Beijing, *Xinhua*, in English, September 8, 2007, *FBIS SOV*, September 8, 2007.

247. Mure Dickie and Jonathan Soble, "Missile Test Fails to Raise China's Ire," *Financial Times*, December 19, 2007, *www. ft.com*; "China Unmoved by Japan Missile Interception," *Reuters*, December 18, 2007.

248. Moscow, *Interfax*, in English, October 17, 2007, *FBIS SOV*, October 17, 2007; Moscow, *Ministry of Foreign Affairs Website, www. mid.ru*, October 17, 2007, *FBIS SOV*, October 17, 2007.

249. *Ibid.;* Tokyo, Japan, *Kyodo World Service*, in English, October 13, 2007, *FBIS SOV*, October 13, 2007.

250. "Russia Against 'Narrow' Asia-Pacific Military-Political Groupings," *RIA Novosti*, July 24, 2008.

251. Moscow, *Interfax*, in English, September 15, 2003, *FBIS SOV*, September 15, 2003.

252. "Russia 'No Longer Uses' Nuclear Sub Deterrent," *United Press International*, April 29, 2008.

253. Open Source Committee, *OSC Report*, in English, *FBIS SOV*, September 7, 2007.

254. Kristian Atland, "The Introduction, Adoption, and Implementation of Russia's 'Northern Strategic Bastion' Concept, 1992-1999," *Journal of Slavic Military Studies*, Vol. X, No. 4, 2007, pp. 499-528; "Russia and Norway's Arctic Challenge, " *Jane's Intelligence Digest*, May 20, 2008.

255. Dmitri Litovkin, "We Didn't Send Him For a Star: A Skif Flew From the North Pole to Kanin Nos," Moscow, *Izvestiya Moscow Edition* in Russian, September 13, 2006, *FBIS SOV*, September 13, 2006.

256. Moscow, *ITAR-TASS*, in English, May 5, 2008, *FBIS SOV*, May 5, 2008; Yuri Gavrilov, "Long-Range Aviation Inhabits Arctic Skies," Moscow, *Rossiyskaya Gazeta*, in Russian, May 15, 2008, *FBIS SOV*, May 15, 2008; Moscow, *IRAR-TASS*, in English, March 20, 2008, *FBIS SOV*, March 20, 2008.

257. Litovkin, "We Didn't Send Him For a Star"; Moscow, *Agentstvo Voyennykh Novostey*, April 9, 2008.

258. "Russia Orders Upgrade of Nuclear Deterrent."

259. Moscow, *Agentstvo Voyennykh Novostey Internet Version*, March 21, 2005, *FBIS SOV*, March 21, 2005.

260. See Sergei Ivanov's remarks in Vladimir Mukhin, "Generals Will Be Obliged to Be Accountable to Inspection by Parents. Defense Minister Initiates New State in Military Reform," Moscow, *Nezavisimaya Gazeta*, in Russian, November 17, 2006, *FBIS SOV*, November 17, 2006.

261. Steve Gutterman, "Russia Could Use Preemptive Nuclear Strikes," *Associated Press*, January 21, 2008.

262. *Ibid.*

263. *Ibid.*

264. Wortzel; Spencer; Zhang, pp. 164-183.

265. Eugene Myasnikov, "Russian Perceptions and Prospects for Nuclear Weapons Reductions in Northeast Asia," *Inesap Bulletin*, No. 24, 2004, *www.inesap.org/bulletin24/art05.htm*.

266 . Moltz, p. 730.

267. Larry M. Wortzel, *China's Nuclear Forces: Operations, Training, Doctrine, Command, Control, and Campaign Planning*, Carlisle, PA: Strategic Studies Institute, U.S. Army War College, 2007; Richard Spencer, "China To Modernize Nuclear Weapons Capability," *London Daily Telegraph*, May 9, 2008; Baohui Zhang, "The Taiwan Strait and the Future of China's No-First-Use Nuclear Policy," *Comparative Strategy*, Vol. XXVII, No. 2, March-April 2008, pp. 164-183.

268. Wortzel; Spencer; Zhang; "Extensive Missile Site in china Revealed by Satellite: analyst," *Space War*, May 15, 2008; "Extensive nuclear Missile Deployment Are a Discovered in Central Asia," posted by Hans Kristensen, May 15, 2008, *www.fas.*

org/blog/ssp/2208//05/extensive-nuclear-deployment-area-discovered-in-central-china.

269. Open Source Committee, *OSC Analysis*: "Russia: Foreign Policy Thinkers Undaunted by Rising China," *FBIS SOV*, September 6, 2007.

270. Aleksandr' Menshikov, "Problems of Russian Antimissile Defense: What It Can and Should Protect Against, And What It Should Not," Moscow, *Vozdushno-Kosmicheskaya Oborona*, in Russian, August 15, 2004, *FBIS SOV*, August 15, 2004.

271. Wortzel; Spencer, Zhang.

272. Tony Halpin, "Putin Confronts US With Threat To Arms Pact," *Times Online*, October 13, 2007, *www.timesonline.co.uk/tol/news/world/europe/article2648440.ece*.

273. Demetri Sevastopulo, Neil Buckley, Daniel Dombey, and Jan Cienski," Russia Threatens To Quit Arms Treaty," *Financial Times*, February 15, 2007, *www.ft.com*.

274. Moscow, *ITAR-TASS*, in English, October 23, 2007, *FBIS SOV*, October 23, 2007.

275. Minxin Pei, "China's Hedged Acquiescence," Byung-Kook Kim and Anthony Jones, eds., *Power and Security in Northeast Asia: Shifting Strategies,* Boulder, CO: Lynne Rienner Publishers, 2007, p. 115; Lukin, pp. 187-193.

276. Lyle Goldstein and Vitaly Kozyrev, "China, Japan, and the Scramble for Siberia," *Survival*, Vol. XLVIII, No. 1, Spring, 2006, pp. 175-176; Kim Yo'ng Hu'i, "The Relevance of Central Asia," Seoul, Korea, *JoongAng Ilbo Internet Version*, in English, July 11, 2005, *FBIS SOV*, July 11, 2005.

277. Davydov, p. 38, Stephen Blank," Strategic Rivalry in the Asia-Pacific Theater: A New Nuclear Arms Race?" *Korean Journal of Defense Analysis*, Vol. XX, No. 1, Spring, 2008, pp. 27-46; Stephen Blank, "New Twists and Turns in Russo-Japanese Relations," Forthcoming; Stephen Blank, "Asia and Russian Energy Under Dmitri Medvedev: What Can Be Expected?" *Northeast Asia Energy Focus*, No. 2, 2008, Forthcoming.

278. Mark Katz, "Exploiting Rivalries for Fun and Profit: An Assessment of Putin's Foreign Policy approach," *Problems of Post-Communism*, Vol. LII, No. 3, May-June, 2005, pp. 25-31; Jonathan D. Pollack, "The Changing-Political Military Environment: Northeast Asia," Zalmay Khalilzad, David T. Oretsky, Jonathan D. Pollack, Kevin L. Pollpeter, Angel Rabassa, David, Shlapak, Abram N. Shulsky, and Ashley J. Tellis, eds., *The United States and Asia: Toward a New U.S. Strategy and Force Posture*, Santa Monica: CA, Rand Corporation, 1997, pp. 113-114.

279. Moscow, *ITAR-TASS*, in English, March 7, 2008, *FBIS SOV*, March 7, 2008; Dmitri Trenin, *Russia's Foreign Policy: Self-Affirmation, or a Tool for Modernization?* Moscow: Carnegie Endowment for Peace, Moscow Center, 2008, *www.carnegie.ru/en/pubs/media/78308.htm*.

280. Glenn C. Buchan, David Matonic, Calvin Shipbaugh, and Richard Mesic, *Future Roles of U.S. Nuclear Forces: Implications for U.S. Strategy*, Santa Monica, CA: Rand Corporation, 2000, p. 15; Joseph Ferguson, "U.S.-Russia Relations: Awaiting the G-8," *Comparative Connections*, June 2006.

281. M. Gareyev, V. Dvorkin, S. A. Kortunov, Iu. Krokunov, V. Kuznetsov, M. Lysenko, S. Rogov, V. Chkhikvishviili, and K. Barskii, "Revolution in Military Matters and Strategic Stability," *International Affairs*, No. 5, 2001, accessed from *www.ciaonet.org*, March 23, 2005 (italics in the original).

282. What Putin Said to Le Monde—In Full," *Russia Today*, June 1, 2008, *www.russiatoday.ru/news/news/25525*.

283. "No Final Decision to Quit INF Treaty—FM Lavrov," *RIA Novosti*, February 16, 2007; "Russia Made a Mistake By Scrapping Its Mid-Range Missiles—Ivanov," Moscow, *Interfax*, in English, February 7, 2007, *FBIS SOV*, February 7, 2007.

284. Moscow, *ITAR-TASS* in English, February 26, 2007, *FBIS SOV*, February 26, 2007.

285. *Ibid.*

286. *Ibid.*

287. Tehran, *Fars News Agency Internet Version*, in Persian, November 27, 2007, *FBIS SOV*, November 27, 2007.

288. Tehran, *Jomhuri-ye Eslami Internet Version*, in Persian, "U.S./ May Station Ballistic Missiles Instead of Interceptors in Poland," Moscow, September 11, 2007, *FBIS SOV* September 11, 2007.

289. *FBIS SOV*, July 8, 2008; Moscow, *Agentstvo Voyennykh Novostey Internet Version*, in English, April 24, 2006, *FBIS SOV*, April 24, 2006.

290. *FBIS SOV* July 26, 2006.

291. *Ibid*; Moscow, *Interfax*, in Russian, July 1, 2008, *FBIS SOV*, July 1, 2008.

292. *Kommersant.com*, in Russian, July 10, 2008, *FBIS SOV*, July 10, 2008.

293. Lilia Shevtsova, "The End of Putin's Era: Domestic Drivers of Foreign Policy," In *U.S.-Russian Relations: Is Conflict Inevitable?* Washington, DC: Hudson Institute, June 26, 2007, p. 50.

294. Conversations with European officials in March-April 2008, who themselves used the term Mafia state to characterize Russia.

295. Michael Binyon, "Drop Your Silly Atlantic Solidarity And Support Us, Putin Tells the West," *Timesonline*, September 15, 2007, *www.timesonline.co.uk/tol/news/world/europe/article/2436902*, accessed on August 2, 2008; "Interview Of President Dmitry Medvedev by Reuters News Agency" June 23, 2008, *www.in.mid.ru*, accessed August 2, 2008.

296. Thayer and Skypek, pp. 61-68; "Upgrade of Nuclear Deterrent Ordered," *Moscow Times*, September 29, 2008; "Opening Address at a Meeting with Commanders of Military Districts," *www.kremlin.ru*, September 26, 2008.

297. Arbatov and Dvorkin; Kortunov, *FBIS SOV*, August 11, 2006.

298. Moscow, *Argumenty if Fakty, Interview with Chief of Staff General Yuri Baluyevsky*, in Russian, June 21, 2005, *FBIS SOV*, June 21, 2005.

299. Simon Saradzhyan, "Military to Get $189BN Overhaul," *Moscow Times*, February 8, 2007; "Russia to Put 50 Topol-M Millie Systems on Duty Before 2015," *RIA Novosti*, February 7, 2007; Vladimir Isachenkov, "Weapons Plan Strives to Beat Soviet Readiness," *Washington Times*, February 8, 2007, p. 13; "Russian Defense Chief Unveils Army Spending Spree," *defensenews.com*, February 8, 2007.

300. Thayer and Skypek, pp. 61-69; "Upgrade of Nuclear Deterrent Ordered"; "Opening Address at a Meeting with Commanders of Military Districts."

301. "Interview With Colonel-General Nikolai Yevgenyevich Solovtsov by Oleg Vasilenko," Moscow, *Armeiskii Sbornik*, in Russian, December, 2007, *FBIS SOV*, July 13, 2008.

302. "Russia Tests New Strategic Weapons As Vice-Premier Rejects Proposals for Increasing the Rate of Weapons Production," *WMD Insights*, February 2008.

303. Kiev, *Zavtra*, in Russian, May 29, 2007, *FBIS SOV*, May 29, 2007.

304. Moscow, *Agentstvo Voyennykh Novostey Internet Version*, in English, February 12, 2004, *FBIS SOV*, February 12, 2004; Moscow, *Agentstvo Voyennykh Novostey, Internet Version* in English, May 26, 2005, *FBIS SOV*, May 26, 2005; "Missile Defense Briefing Report," American Foreign Policy Council, No. 176, May 9, 2005; Shumikhin, p. 5; Moscow, *Krasnaya Zvezda*, in Russian, February 25, 2004, *FBIS SOV*, February 25, 2004; Moscow, *Izvestiya*, in Russian, February 21, 2004; *FBIS SOV*, February 21, 2004.

305. Moscow, *RTR TV*, in Russian, February 18, 2004, *FBIS SOV*, February 18, 2004; Moscow, *Agentstvo Voyennykh Novostey*,

Internet Version, in Russian, December 13, 2007, *FBIS SOV*, December 13, 2007.

306. Stephen J. Cimbala, "Russia's Vanishing Sea-Based Deterrent?: Implications and Cautions," Unpublished Manuscript, cited by permission of the author.

307. *Ibid.,* citing "Russia May Deploy New-Generation Ballistic Missiles by 2017," *RIA Novosti*, December 14, 2007.

308. "Upgrade of Nuclear Deterrent Ordered"; "Opening Address at a Meeting with Commanders of Military Districts."

309. Moscow, *Interfax*, in Russian, July 9, 2008, *FBIS SOV*, July 9, 2008.

310. Viktor Litovkin, "General Gareyev, Rossiia Menyaet Svoiu Voyennomu Doktrinu," *RIA Novosti*, January 18, 2007, cited in Igor Khripunov, "How Safe is Russia?: Public Risk Perception and Nuclear Security," *Problems of Post-Communism,* Vol. LIV, No. 5, September-October, 2007, p. 25.

311. Moscow, *Novyy Region Internet*, in Russian, November 14, 2007, Nikolay Poroskov, "In Thrall to a Myth: The Russian Army: Revival or Degradation?" Moscow, *Vremya Novostey*, February 22, 2008, *FBIS SOV*, February 22, 2008.

312. Dmitri Trenin, *Toward a New Euro-Atlantic "Hard" Security Agenda, Prospects for Trilateral U.S.-EU-Russia Cooperation, Europe, Russia and the United States Finding a New Balance*, Washington, DC: IFRI and CSIS, 2008, *www.csis.org*, or *www.ifri.org*, 2008, p. 11.

313. Hans M. Kristensen, "The Role of U.S. Nuclear Weapons: New Doctrine Falls Short of Bush Pledge," *www.armscontrol.org/ node/1875/print*, accessed August 4, 2008; Hans M. Kristensen, "US Strategic War Planning After 9/11: Trends and Options for Change," Presentation to the Monterey Institute of International Studies, July 24, 2007, *www.fas.org* or *www.nukestrat.com*; Ivan Oelrich, *Missions for Nuclear Weapons After the Cold War*, Occasional Paper No. 3, Federation of American Scientists, 2005; Joint Publication 3-12, *Doctrine for Joint Nuclear Operations*, Washington

DC, Chairman of the Joint Chiefs of Staff, 2005, pp. xi, II, 2, 8-9, 12-13, III, 2-3; *Deterrence Operations Joint Operating Concept*, Version 2.0, Washington, DC: Department of Defense, 2006, pp. 40-41.

314. J. D. Crouch, *Special Briefing on the Nuclear Posture Review*, Washington, DC: U.S. Department of Defense, Office of the Assistant Secretary of Defense, January 9, 2002, *www.defrenselink. mil/transcripts/transcript.aspx?transcriptid=1108.*

315. *Ibid.*

316. "Mikhail Tsypkin, "Russian Politics, Policymaking and American Missile Defense," Forthcoming (made available to me by Dr. Tsypkin).

317. *Ibid.*

318. "U.S. National Space Policy," Washington, DC: Office of the President, the White House, August 31, 2006, *www.globalsecurity. org/space/library/policy/national/us-space-policy_060831.htm.*

319. William Arkin, "Not Just a Last Resort?" *Washington Post*, May 15, 2005, p. B01; McDonough, *Nuclear Superiority*; Lieber and Press, "The Rise of U.S. Nuclear Primacy," pp. 42-54; Lieber and Press, "The End of MAD?: The Nuclear Dimensions of U.S. Primacy," pp. 7-44; Bunn and Chyba, eds., Jonathan Schell, *The Seventh Decade; The New Shape of Nuclear Danger*, New York: Metropolitan Books, Henry Holt & Co., 2007, pp. 112-134; Hans M. Kristensen, *Global Strike: A Chronology of the Pentagon's New Offensive Strike Plan*, Washington, DC: Federation of American Scientists, 2006; Hans M. Kristensen, "The Role of U.S. Nuclear Weapons: New Doctrine Falls Short of Bush Pledge," *www. armscontrol.org/node/1875/print*, accessed August 4, 2008; Hans M. Kristensen, "US Strategic War Planning After 9/11: Trends and Options for Change," Presentation to the Monterey Institute of International Studies, July 24, 2007, *www.fas.org* or *www.nukestrat. com*; Ivan Oelrich, *Missions for Nuclear Weapons After the Cold War*, Occasional Paper No. 3, Federation of American Scientists, 2005; Joint Publication, 3-12 *Doctrine for Joint Nuclear Operations*, Washington, DC: Chairman of the Joint Chiefs of Staff, 2005, pp. xi, II, 2, 8-9, 12-13, III, 2-3; *Deterrence Operations Joint Operating Concept*, Version 2.0, Washington, DC: Department of Defense, 2006, pp. 40-41.

320. "Chinese Nuclear Arsenal Increased by 25 Percent Since 2006, Pentagon Report Indicates," Blog Posted by Hans Kristensen March 6, 2008, *www.fas.org/blog/ssp/2008/03/chinese_nuclear_arsenal_increa.pho/print*, accessed on August 5, 2008.

321. "Tekst Voyennaya Doktrina Rossiiskoi Federatsii," *Nezavisimaya Gazeta,* April 22, 2000.

322. Cimbala, "Russia's Vanishing Sea-Based Deterrent?"

323. *Ibid.*

324. Cimbala, *The New Nuclear Disorder.*

325. Robert Manning, Brad Roberts, and Ronald Montaperto, *China, Nuclear Weapons, and Arms Control: A Council Paper*, New York: Council on Foreign Relations, 2000.

326. Moscow, *RIA Novosti*, in English, August 5, 2008, *FBIS SOV*, August 5, 2008.

327. Joseph Cirincione, "The Asian Nuclear Reaction Chain," *Foreign Policy*, Spring, 2000.

328. Stephen Blank, *Towards a New Russia Policy,* pp. 69-108.

329. Tesmur Basilia, "Eurasian Commentary," Jan H, Kalicki and Eugene K. Lawson, eds., *Russian-Eurasian Renaissance?: U.S. Trade and Investment in Russia and Eurasia*, Stanford, CA: Stanford University Press, 2003, p. 166.

330. Dmitry Furman, "A Silent Cold War," *Russia in Global Affairs*, Vol. IV, No. 2, April-June, 2006, p. 72.

331. Ibid., p. 73.

332. "Putin Speaks Out Against "Exporting Capitalist Democracy," *ITAR-TASS News Agency*, April 11, 2003, retrieved from Lexis-Nexis; for an example from Turkmenistan, see Gennady Sysoev, "Saparmyrat Niyazov Seeks Protection,"

Moscow, *Kommersant*, in Russian, April 11, 2003, *FBIS SOV*, April 11, 2003.

333. Basilia, p. 163.

334. Garry Kasparov, "What's Bad for Putin Is Best for Russians," *New York Times*, July 10, 2006.

335. Sten Rynning, "Peripheral or Powerful? The European Union's Strategy to Combat the Proliferation of Nuclear Weapons," *European Security*, Vol. XVI, No. 3-4, September-December 2007, p. 270.

336. *Ibid.*

337. *Ibid;* Jones, pp. 3-16.

338. Rynning, p. 271.

339. *Ibid.*, p. 275.

340. McDonough, *Nuclear Superiority*; Lieber and Press, "The Rise of U.S. Nuclear Primacy," pp. 42-54; Keir A. Lieber and Daryl G. Press, "The End of MAD?: The Nuclear Dimensions of U.S. Primacy," pp. 7-44; Bunn and Chyba, eds.

341. Rynning, p. 275; Justin Bernier, "The Death of Disarmament in Russia?" *Parameters*, Vol. XXXIV, No. 2, Summer 2004, pp. 84-103.

342. Stephen J. Cimbala, "Missile Defense and Mother Russia: Scarecrow or Showstopper?" *European Security*, Vol. XVI, No. 3-4, September-December, 2007, p. 294.

343. One need only cite Russian interventions in the Caucasus, Moldova, an endless Chechen war that has now spread to the North Caucasus and the bizarre intervention in Kosovo in 1999.

344. Robert Wright, "An American Foreign Policy That Both Realists and Idealists Should Fall in Love With," *New York Times*, July 16, 2006, pp. E12-13.

345. *Ibid.*

346. Stephen Blank, "Russia's Project 2008: Reforming the Army and Preparing a Coup," *World Affairs,* Fall 2006, pp. 65-79.

347. Michael Mainville, "Armed Clash With Georgia Feared," *Washington times,* June 21, 2006, p. 14; Stephen Blank, "Russia Versus NATO in the CIS," *Radio Free Europe Radio Liberty,* May 14, 2008.

348. Alexander Golts and Tonya Putnam, "State Militarism and Its Legacies: Why Military Reform Has Failed in Russia," *International Security,* Vol. XXIX, No. 2, Fall, 2004, pp. 121-159; Aleksandr' Golts, *Armiya Rossii: 11 Poteryannykh Let,* Moscow, Zakharov, 2004.

BIOGRAPHICAL SKETCH OF THE AUTHOR

STEPHEN J. BLANK has served as the Strategic Studies Institute's expert on the Soviet bloc and the post-Soviet world since 1989. Prior to that he was Associate Professor of Soviet Studies at the Center for Aerospace Doctrine, Research, and Education, Maxwell Air Force Base, and taught at the University of Texas, San Antonio, and at the University of California, Riverside. Dr. Blank is the editor of *Imperial Decline: Russia's Changing Position in Asia*, coeditor of *Soviet Military and the Future*, and author of *The Sorcerer as Apprentice: Stalin's Commissariat of Nationalities, 1917-1924*. He has also written many articles and conference papers on Russian, Commonwealth of Independent States, and Eastern European security issues. Dr. Blank's current research deals with proliferation and the revolution in military affairs, and energy and security in Eurasia. His two most recent books are *Russo-Chinese Energy Relations: Politics in Command*, London: Global Markets Briefing, 2006; and *Natural Allies?: Regional Security in Asia and Prospects for Indo-American Strategic Cooperation*, Carlisle Barracks, PA: Strategic Studies Institute, U.S. Army War College, 2005. He holds a B.A. in History from the University of Pennsylvania, and a M.A. and Ph.D. in History from the University of Chicago.